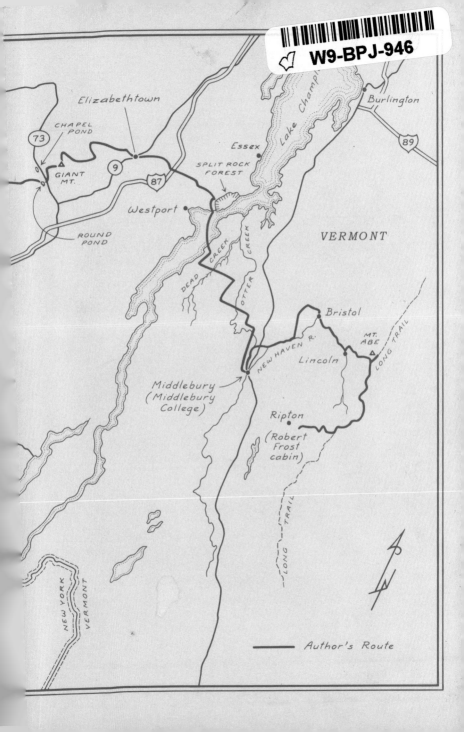

W9-BPJ-946

——— Author's Route

Wandering Home

Also in the Crown Journeys Series

Land's End: A Walk in Provincetown
by Michael Cunningham

*After the Dance: A Walk Through Carnival in
Jacmel, Haiti* by Edwidge Dandicat

City of the Soul: A Walk in Rome
by William Murray

*Washington Schlepped Here: Walking in the Nation's
Capital* by Christopher Buckley

Hallowed Ground: A Walk at Gettysburg
by James M. McPherson

Fugitives and Refugees: A Walk in Portland, Oregon
by Chuck Palahniuk

Blues City: A Walk in Oakland
by Ishmael Reed

Time and Tide: A Walk Through Nantucket
by Frank Conroy

*Lost in My Own Backyard: A Walk in Yellowstone
National Park* by Tim Cahill

Never a City So Real: A Walk in Chicago
by Alex Kotlowitz

*The Great Psychedelic Armadillo Picnic:
A "Walk" in Austin* by Kinky Friedman

Time's Magpie: A Walk in Prague
by Myla Goldberg

ALSO BY BILL McKIBBEN

Enough

Long Distance

Hundred Dollar Holiday

Maybe One

Hope, Human and Wild

The Comforting Whirlwind

The Age of Missing Information

The End of Nature

A Long Walk Across

America's Most Hopeful Landscape:

Vermont's Champlain Valley and

New York's Adirondacks

Wandering Home

Bill McKibben

CROWN JOURNEYS

CROWN PUBLISHERS · NEW YORK

A list of permissions appears on page 158.

Published in the United States by Crown Journeys, an imprint of the Crown Publishing Group, a division of Random House, Inc., New York.
www.crownpublishing.com

CROWN JOURNEYS *and the Crown Journeys colophon are trademarks of Random House, Inc.*

Library of Congress Cataloging-in-Publication Data
McKibben, Bill.
Wandering home: a long walk across America's most hopeful landscape:
Vermont's Champlain Valley and New York's Adirondacks/
Bill McKibben.—1st ed.
1. Adirondack Mountains (N.Y.)—Description and travel.
2. Champlain Valley—Description and travel.   3. Vermont—
Description and travel.   4. Adirondack Mountains (N.Y.)—Social life
and customs.   5. Champlain Valley—Social life and customs.
6. Vermont—Social life and customs.   7. McKibben, Bill—Travel—
New York (State)—Adirondack Mountains.   8. McKibben, Bill—
Travel—Champlain Valley.   9. Hiking—New York (State)—
Adirondack Mountains.   10. Hiking—Champlain Valley.   I. Title. II.
Crown Journeys series

| *F127.A2M357* | *2005* |
| *917.47'5—dc22* | *2004016455* |

ISBN 0-609-61073-2

Printed in the United States of America

DESIGN BY LAUREN DONG
MAP BY JACKIE AHER

10 9 8 7 6 5 4 3 2 1

First Edition

For Nick, Jackie, Gary, and Kathy on the west,
and John, Rita, Warren, and Barry in the east.

MY MOOD WAS DARKER THAN IT SHOULD HAVE been for the start of a journey. For one thing, I had packed too heavy; the stove, the pad, the water filter, the tent that would make my camp theoretically comfortable, were for the moment making my shoulders actually sore and my knees actually ache. And I hiked in a cloud—no views, just a soggy mist. The trail—Vermont's Long Trail—ran up and down like a giant's EKG, farther than my rather too cursory glance at the map had led me to expect. I'd taken an easy fall romp with a daypack along this path the year before, and remembered dimly that a field of ferns marked the approach of camp—now, heavy-laden, I walked through just such a fern field ten times in the course of the afternoon, each time more certain that this must be the one. But no, and no, and no, and no. Not until dinnertime, with ten solid hours of walking behind me, did I arrive, sore-footed, calf-cramped, and more than a little uncertain about the weeks of walking that lay ahead, at a small lean-to 750 feet beneath the summit of Mount Abraham, Vermont's third-highest peak.

I sprawled out on top of my sleeping bag and commenced infusing sandwiches into my system. As I proceeded, the fog started to clear, and with it my funk. So I dug an extra layer from my pack and decided, after several moment's hesitation, that I still had energy enough for the 20-minute climb to the top of the peak and the sunset view. It was, as it turned out, one of the better decisions of my life.

Mount Abraham—Mount Abe to its neighbors—commands a 360-degree view. South and north, the narrow ridge of the Green Mountains stretches off toward Killington and Camel's Hump respectively. To the east, the vista stretches easily across Vermont, barely fifty miles wide at this point, and into New Hampshire's White Mountains—on a clear day you can make out Mount Washington. But most times, and especially tonight, the western vista demands the most attention. Lake Champlain lies in the middle distance, gleaming like a sheet of gold foil in the late sun. It runs 125 miles from south of Ticonderoga to north of the Canadian border. Fourteen miles wide at its broadest, 400 feet deep at its deepest, Champlain is America's sixth-largest lake. (Not Great, but great). Behind it, the jumbled High Peaks of the

Adirondacks rise hard and fast, 5,000 feet above the lake—as fast and as far as the Wasatch above Salt Lake or the Rockies over Boulder. And in the foreground spreads the broad and fertile Vermont valley that lies between the Greens and the lakeshore.

Tonight a scrim of rain clouds advanced toward me, a gauzy curtain of gray that only made the lake and mountains behind gleam the shinier. It was clearly about to rain, but the worst of it seemed set to pass just north and south; a slight gap in the line headed toward my perch on Mount Abe. Hearing no thunder, I stayed put, and sure enough, the cloud washed up over me. For a few moments, even as the world turned gray, I could still make out the reflecting mirror of the lake; finally it too vanished and all was gloom. But then, even more quickly than it had descended, the cloud swept through, and behind it the world was created fresh. No scrim now, just the fields, the lake, the peaks. When a double rainbow suddenly appeared, it was almost too much—a Disney overdose of glory. But then a rainbow pillar rose straight into the southern sky, and east of that a vaporous twin appeared, and then a kind of rainbow cloud to the north. Soon seven rainbows at once. Then the sun reached just the right angle so that the mist whipping up the face of the peak flashed into clouds of color as it washed over me: a rose cloud, a cloud of green. And always behind it the same line of lake, the same jag of mountain. All at once it struck me, struck me hard, that this was one of those few scenes I would replay in my mind when I someday lay dying.

When I lay living, too—for the territory revealed this evening, the view west from this pinnacle, was the turf of my adult life. To the south I could see the Vermont mountain town of Ripton, set at 1,500 feet, hard against the western spine of the Greens. I'd stepped off this morning from my house there, which we built a few years back, on land once owned by Robert Frost. A quarter-mile through the woods I'd passed the writing cabin where he'd spent his last thirty summers, stocking our cupboard of Yankee imagery with his woodsmen and hill-farmers and sleigh drivers. Now that New Hampshire's Old Man of the Mountain has crashed into granite smithereens, surely Frost's white-haired, craggy visage is New England's most iconic face.

But to the distant west I could see, or so I told myself, Crane Mountain, the peak in whose shadow I'd spent most of my adult life. Forget New England—Crane lies smack in the center of New York's vast Adirondack wilderness. I have a house there, too, also set at 1,500 feet, and it was where I was bound on this walk. Seventy miles, perhaps, as the crow flies, but a couple of hundred on my planned route, which unfolded below me in the dazzling dusk.

I've not moved far in my life. But fairly few people have had the chance to know both sides of this lake with any real closeness. Anyone with the good fortune to own two houses would logically have one at the beach and one in the mountains, or one in the city and one in the country—I know that. But I've not been able to drag myself away from this small corner of the planet. To me, this country on either side of Lake Champlain, though it has no name and appears on no map as a single unit, constitutes one of the world's few great regions, a place more complete, and more full of future promise, than any other spot in the American atlas.

This region (Adimont? The Verandacks?) includes the fertile farms and small woodlots directly beneath me in the Champlain Valley, where a new generation of settlers is trying to figure out new ways to responsibly inhabit the land—ways to farm and log and invest that enrich in the fullest sense of the word. It encompasses the fine small city of Burlington to the north. And across the lake it is made whole by the matchless eastern wilderness of the Adirondacks, the largest park in the lower forty-eight, 6 million acres, bigger than Glacier, Grand Canyon, Yellowstone, and Yosemite combined. At the risk of hyperbole and chauvinism, let me state it plainly: in my experience, the world contains no finer blend of soil and rock and water and forest than that found in this scene laid out before me—a few just as fine, perhaps, but none finer. And no place where the essential human skills—cooperation, husbandry, restraint—offer more possibility for competent and graceful inhabitation, for working out the answers to the questions that the planet is posing in this age of ecological pinch and social fray.

My walk will carry me across this range of mountains—this range of possibilities. I'll go through the back roads of the Champlain Valley and the high passes of the Adirondacks, and through the plans and dreams and accomplishments of loggers and farmers and economists and biologists. I can see most of my route laid out before me tonight as the rainbows fade in the last light, and—sore calves be damned—I can't wait to dive in. Tired as I am, sleep takes a while to come.

In the flatter light of midmorning (for, once asleep, I *slept*), the view is still beautiful, but more daunting. Though to me this wide expanse looks so like a whole, that's only because unlikely circumstance has let me know all of it with some intimacy. For most of the residents of either side, the lake divides it neatly into two very different kingdoms of the imagination. Champlain acts as the border between Vermont and New York, which is not like the border between, say, Connecticut and Massachusetts, or Kansas and Nebraska. This line is rarely crossed. Partly that's because most places you need to take a ferry, but much more because the ferry connects two different states of mind. On one side you stand in "New England," and you can still feel the ocean at your back, and maybe even Olde England beyond that. To a New Englander, Boston is *the city*—the radio mast a couple of peaks north from Mount Abe carries the Red

Sox out across this valley on a summer eve. New England comes with as many icons as Holland—even here, 140 miles from saltwater, the lobster somehow still seems native. The towns tend toward neatness, gathering themselves around white churches—Congregational churches, governing themselves without the aid of bishops or the overly active intervention of the Holy Spirit. And town halls, with their March rite of town meeting—of good, crisp self-governance. It is a tidy place, New England.

Whereas, across the lake, the unruliness of the rest of America begins. Looking west from the top of Mount Abe, you look *West*. For a long time, New Englanders averted their eyes. Mount Marcy, New York, the region's tallest peak, shows up clearly even from the valley towns of Addison County, which were settled in the 1600s. But not until 1834, with Lewis and Clark home for a generation from the Pacific, did a white man bother to go climb it, and he came from downstate New York. Even now, the hikers and climbers of Vermont are more likely to stick to their narrow and relatively crowded mountain trails than to venture to the Adirondacks (there you're far more likely to meet adventurous Quebecois, who have crossed an honest-to-God border for their day's outing). A few years ago, conservationists seeking public support to protect a broad swath of land from Maine to the Great Lakes, commissioned focus groups in Boston, Vermont, and New Hampshire. Testing different formulations, they found that participants didn't want New England to be lumped in with anything New York or even "North-eastern." New England was "serene," "bucolic." "Every-thing is so elegant," said one Boston woman. "It's a very classic place to live."

Indeed they are right to perceive a difference. Cross the lake and you leave behind the neat town green with the bandstand in favor of a more Appalachian look: Methodists and Baptists and Catholics. No one goes to a town meeting—political power and patronage tend to pass on dynastically. There's poverty on both sides of the lake, but somehow it looks rawer on the Adirondack shore, the trailers more numerous and nearer the main road. Boston is suddenly no closer than Detroit. Ver-mont, too, seems distant, all the way across the lake, a mythical land of Saab-driving, goat-cheese-eating Demo-crats. The Adirondacks are higher, colder, and wilder—people have lived here for fewer centuries in fewer numbers, and have never been able to make farming work for long. And so, over time, huge chunks have been left to rewild themselves, till in places it approaches the primeval.

YET IT SEEMS to me they belong together, this Cham-plain Valley of Vermont and this great Adirondack woods. Every bird guide, every alumni association, every corporate sales office considers one shore New England and the other the "mid-Atlantic." But if you stand on top of Mount Abe and huck west, your gob will find its way into the lake and then north into the mighty St. Lawrence—a fur-trading river, flowing out into the bergy Atlantic north at the tip of the Gaspé Peninsula. Wild country. This crest of the Green Mountains is the last upwelling of the coastal geology, the last fold pushed up the colliding plates of the Atlantic shore; on its western slope you face the geology of midcontinent, the Canadian Shield. Once you've started down into the Champlain Valley, you really have begun the journey west.

They have so much to teach each other, these two sides: New Englanders have learned a great deal, mostly through trial and error, about how to successfully inhabit a land, experiments that continue to this day; and Adirondackers, often against their will, have learned as much about how to leave land alone. The distinction is easy to overdraw—Vermont, too, has stopped farming many of its acres, seen a smaller-scale reversion to the wild. The Adirondacks have seen an influx of tourists and retirees from the overdeveloped world to the south. And yet their dual personalities remain surprisingly intact—though roughly the same size as Vermont, the Adirondacks have one-fifth the population, with all that implies. And those two casts of mind, those two sets of skills, are rare, complementary, and extremely useful as we enter this strained century. In most places real husbandry and real wilderness are both disappearing, melted away by the economic sun of industrial efficiency and consumer ease. But neither side of Lake Champlain is yet thoroughly suburbanized, and so these two shores offer some countercultural ideas about what might be, and some poignant reminders about how we once lived.

The sun is high, starting to bear down harder as the morning ebbs. And that's enough airy mountaintop speculation for an entire volume. Time now, on aching calves, to descend the Battell trail down toward civilization. Time to begin the walk west.

LINCOLN, THE TOWN that lies beneath Mount Abe, may be the most picturesque in Vermont (if you needed to remake *The Sound of Music,* you could do it here), and among the most isolated. The only road east, a dirt track that climbs steeply through a mountain gap, is closed half the year by snow. The rest of the time, what traffic there is funnels to the west through another narrow gap on the route I'm walking today.

It's hot, and my lope has turned into a meander. I pass the Weed Farm, a little herb nursery presided over by my daughter's fourth-grade teacher and his partner, who gives my daughter piano lessons. Just down the hill there's the general store, the town library, the white clapboard community church—you might as well be walking through an LL Bean catalog. It's Ur–New England, with all the community virtues that implies: when the New Haven River flooded a few springs ago, it surged through the tiny local library. Almost all the books were lost—every last one of the picture books, down on the low shelves for the kids. But half the town showed up to shovel out the mud and fork the piles of soggy fiction into hay wagons for burial. And when local author Chris Bohjalian told the story in the *Boston Globe* magazine, *Reader's Digest* picked it up as a picturesque example of rural life; soon cartons of new books were arriving from across the country. Everyone in town gave what they could; now there's a handsome new library, a little farther from the river. This spring's fundraiser: a raffle where you have to guess the birth date, weight, and sex of the first lamb born this season.

Such intense charm carries its own dangers, of course. As I walk, my eye keeps returning to a hilltop overlooking the town, where some outlander has cleared a patch and then, as if from a spaceship, plunked down a "home" huge enough to be a junior high school. You can see it from everywhere, the first of many graphic reminders along my route that the scale of this region—herb farms, piano teaching, general stores, little libraries—coexist uneasily with the high-octane national economy, and that hence the values and practices of community come inevitably up against the hyperindividualism of our time, the hyperindividualism that thinks nothing of ruining everyone else's view with a house four times too large for any conceivable purpose. I can feel myself starting to heat up from the inside—this is a sermon I've preached before, and once it gets rolling it's hard to stop—so I find a shallow pool in the New Haven River and lie down for a good cold soak.

My destination tonight is the larger town of Bristol, most of the way down to the valley floor. The last mile or so, the road descends through a tight draw between the Bristol Cliffs wilderness and the towering bluff wall that locals call Deer Leap; since there's only room for the road and the river, I thread my way along the shoulder in the heat, counting Subarus. (Subarus are to Vermont what bicycles were once to Beijing, so nearly ubiquitous that it's impossible to recognize your neighbor by his vehicle. The supermarket parking lot might as well be a Subaru dealership.) As the state road turns toward town, it passes an enormous boulder, what a geologist would call an erratic, left here by the departing glaciers. On it someone long ago carved the Lord's Prayer—apparently because the teamsters tended to use less-than-Christian language as they maneuvered their loads around this tight curve. It's a pleasure to be walking by instead of driving, slow enough to savor the rhythm of the familiar words.

And a greater pleasure to be taking my pack off on the broad side porch of John and Rita Elder's maple-shaded Bristol home, to sit down on their porch swing and unlace my boots. I stretch for a few moments before I knock, close my eyes and savor the sense of, as Isaac Newton would say, a body coming to rest. This was not my home, of course, but I knew the Elders would make me feel like it was—anyway, arriving on foot gives one a slight proprietary sense. It's not like arriving in the car for a dinner party. On foot you arrive late or early, without excuse, and settle into whatever conversation is under way. It took you a while to get there, so you're obviously going to stay awhile. It feels like *visiting* in an older sense of the word, and you bring with you the news of the road, not the news you heard on *All Things Considered*.

I'd planned the first part of my route around this house, for John and Rita are among my favorite people, and John is the great writer of these few mountains, this small valley. Not that he's from here—like Robert Frost, he's from California. He grew up to be a literature professor, and moved in the there's-a-job-open fashion of academics to Middlebury College in the early 1970s, never intending to stay. "We always figured we'd eventually go back to the West," he says. But like many of us he found himself falling under the spell of the new breed of nature writers whose great teaching was *place:* Barry Lopez, Ed Abbey, Wendell Berry. (His particular guru was the poet Gary Snyder.) Just as important, John was falling under the spell of the Green Mountains. Before long he was teaching one of the college's most popular courses—"Visions of Nature." His seminars and symposiums originally met in classrooms—but increasingly on mountaintops and by the shores of ponds, and in the spreading fields of the college's Bread Loaf campus, Frost's old summer haunt.

Elder—tall, skinny, goofy warm smile, constant twinkle—nonetheless lives up to his name. He has an innate and generous sobriety, an earnestness a little out of place even in the not-very-cynical world of Middlebury College. You want to be thinking your least selfish thoughts in his company, which is what we mean, I guess, when we say that someone "brings out the best in you." And more and more he was trying to bring out the best in the land around him. After years of describing these slopes and pastures, he's begun to work the land as well.

Which is why in the morning I left my pack on his porch and headed off for a morning of labor in his sugar-bush, a hundred acres of prime maple woods in nearby Starksboro. With his sons Matthew and Caleb, he's built a stout sugarhouse near the bottom of the land, and now he's ready to put in a bigger boiling pan, allowing him to expand his operation from 175 to 500 taps. Today we're hauling out the old plastic tubing that drains the spiles and carries the sap down to the evaporator. It's companionable work, especially since John interrupts it every few minutes to show off some particular delight: "There's blue cohosh, and that's maidenhair fern," he says. "They indicate lime-rich soil. So does that plantain-leaved sedge. We counted thirty-one species of wild-flower up here one day." The slope was likely clearcut sixty or seventy years ago, but the rich soils have bred another stand of big trees. And now it won't be clearcut again, not ever; earlier that week, John and Rita had donated a conservation easement on the land to the Vermont Nature Conservancy, assuring it would never be developed—except for two small house lots, one for each son. "See those huge ice-wedged erratics over there? That's where Rita and I want our ashes scattered."

Driving back to Bristol in his pickup with the old tubing piled in back, we pass example after example of just the kind of careful reinhabitation he's been promoting. On the northeastern edge of town, for instance, a tidy farm occupies the one broad stretch of flat land. A group of Elder's neighbors have been trying, thus far unsuccessfully, to buy the land because it would serve as a natural plug on further sprawl. To pay off the note, they'd need to lease some of the land for a community-supported agriculture farm, an ecologically sound woodlot, perhaps a fishery on the brook that flows through. On the ridge above the land, the same group of neighbors is trying something even more exciting: the Community Equity Project is helping buy a big piece of timberland, and then selling shares in the property, allowing residents without much cash to become joint owners and managers of the landscape. If they have no cash but own a backhoe, they can help maintain the skid roads and pull logs out— sweat equity will do. All of the logging will be done according to the strictest set of environmental criteria. So, no second homes sprout, local people find work and ownership, the forest flourishes.

Back in town, we head for the Bristol landfill. A few other guys in pickups are unloading debris, and so is the town's sole garbage truck, a flatbed pulled by a phlegmatic pair of Percheron draft horses. Their driver bid low for the town contract a few years ago, and ever since then he's ranged the town's compact streets, picking up trash bags and recycling bins. The team walks at a pace that lets him load easily—indeed, he can usually count on the assistance of one or another young girl eager for the chance to be near the massive team. We came home, washed up, and then headed out for the short walk to dinner at Bristol's new Bobcat Café, built with money loaned by community residents. Many of the financiers were lined up at the bar, enjoying their 25 percent discount on the Bobcat's home-brewed beer. Do you see what I mean? People are *trying* things here.

And so to bed—it wasn't precisely the same glow I'd felt in the sunset on Mount Abe, but it was a glow nonetheless.

LIKE JOHN, I am primarily a writer. We are, that is, good with words, verbally dexterous, jugglers of symbols. And so we have a role to play helping to nudge our communities toward some more reasonable path, toward something that might not rely quite as deeply on the environmental ruination of cheap oil, on the human ruination of cheap labor. We can coax, we can alarm, we can point to possibilities. But let's face it—the Western world is knee-deep in symbol-manipulators right now. We verbally facile folk form an enormous tribe—throw a rock in Vermont and you'll hit a published author, who will let out some creative oath. What we need more of are people who actually know what they're doing out in the physical world— who know so well that they can not just carry forward old tradition but work out new and better ways of doing things. And so the next morning I resumed my walk again, this time in the company of one of John's neighbors, a man named David Brynn.

Oddly enough, Brynn is tall and skinny, too, with a smile about as sunny as Elder's. He grew up just across the border in Massachusetts, but swears he was conceived in Montpelier, Vermont's capital; his wife, Louise, is a sixth-generation Bristolite. He studied forestry in school, and now serves as the Addison County forester—but he's never been swallowed up by the industry status quo. He founded a group called Vermont Family Forests (VFF) in his spare time, and many of the best ideas in this slice of Vermont sprang full grown from his brain. Or sprang half-baked—he has plenty of colleagues, who help make real his multitude of visions.

So it's always a pleasure to walk with him in the woods. There's guaranteed to be a mix of down-to-earth and pie-in—well, pie hovering in midair, not yet quite in reach but getting closer. When he ventures onto a woodlot, oddly, trees seem to be the last thing he notices.

Instead, it's the condition of the logging roads: have they been built away from steep slopes, for instance, and with enough waterbars to keep soil from eroding? "I get emotionally involved with broad-based dips," he says this morning as we stroll. "There's a formula to getting them right. You divide 1,000 by the grade, and that's where you need them—so this is a 7-percent grade, you need a dip every 140 feet. Yes! Right here! We're going to get a deluge this afternoon, and there will be water on this surface, but there won't be any erosion."

Once the thrill of road maintenance subsides, however, it's clear he can see the forest, too. We haven't been walking five minutes when he drops his voice, motions me off the trail, and leads me to a little grove. "These are two of my favorite white oaks on earth," he says, patting a pair of lovely straight trees. "I get goose bumps when I come over here, and I'm getting them now."

VFF enrolls woodlot owners who agree to follow the program's strict ecological standards—not just about sound road building, but leaving lots of dead trees as standing snags for wildlife, staying far away from streams, and a hundred other details. The guidelines fill a thick manual, but of course there's a rub: building all those waterbars and broad-based dips takes longer than cutting an eroding track straight to the trees you want to harvest. It takes longer to be responsible, in logging as in every other thing on the Earth. And time is money, so in some sense bad logging is efficient.

Brynn's basic task, then, is not just figuring out how many trees you need to leave standing for birds' nests—it's figuring out how to increase the return to landowners and loggers so that they can afford to be responsible. "We find bare-bones logging around here costs $150 per thousand board feet, and doing it the right way costs $220 to $260 per thousand board feet. So we had to come up with some way to pay for that difference." VFF has played with many schemes to make up that gap; most of them come down, in the end, to eliminating some of the middlemen and to branding the wood as local and sustainable so that people will pay a slight premium. "Right now the Vermont timber industry is worth more than a billion dollars, but stumpage—the money paid to the guy who owns the woodlot—is only 3 percent of that. It's exactly the same as growing potatoes for McDonald's. You're completely at the mercy of the mill."

But localizing the timber supply is just half the battle. The other half is convincing consumers that what they want in their homes is the same thing that the forest wants to yield. A few years ago, for instance, Middlebury College decided to erect a vast new science building, Bicentennial Hall. The architects specified, as architects usually do, that the interior wood be "Grade 1"—by the standards of the Architectural Woodwork Institute, that means it should be uniform in color and grain, with few "flaws." That kind of wood, though, comes only from big trees with few knot-forming side branches, and removing those trees from the forest ("high-grading" is what the loggers call it) has left the forests of the Northeast filled with smaller and weaker trees. It's as if we were some species of wolf that, instead of culling the sick and the feeble, only went for prey in its prime. The alternative is to decide, as Middlebury College did, that what you used to think of as flaws could be reimagined as *character.* "That tree has been standing there two hundred years, taking whatever nature can fling at it," says Brynn. "That's not a problem, that's an asset." If you walked through Bicentennial Hall, you'd immediately see what he was talking about, for the walls are filled with little streaks and swirls and flickers that please the eye like the dance of flames in a fireplace. Before long you're beginning to think in other ways that used to be heresy—like, why does my floor have to be all one type of wood, a big expanse of unbroken oak? Why can't it be like the forest that surrounds us, which is roughly equal parts birch and beech and maple? VFF supplied the timber for the home we built in Ripton a few years ago: local wood, local mill, local carpenters. It looks beautiful to the eye, and to the mind's eye, too, because I can walk you to the forest it came from and show you that it's still intact. Show you the broad-based dips.

If you can make the economics work, then there's a chance the people who won the woodlot won't sell it for subdivisions. Brynn and I reach the edge of the forest and peer off into a new clearcut with a nice orange No Trespassing sign. "This was a beautiful forest. But the owner has cashed out, and he's going to put in houses. And the people who buy them—well, they'll be here a couple of years and then we'll come up to do a new cut so this guy can net enough money to keep his forest intact, and those new owners will be outraged we're cutting trees."

"It's never going to be a huge wildland here," Brynn says as we come to the edge of this small forest. "It's always going to be more of a patchwork quilt. But there are so many people who could develop a positive experience with their piece of the quilt. See this stump? A beautiful white pine, shot straight up, not a pimple on it. Then it got blister rust, right about the same time that the Lake Champlain Maritime Museum came looking for clear white pine for the mast of a replica pilot gig they were building. The schoolkids who were doing the work came out here, one cold day in December, to harvest it. They weren't the luckiest kids—a lot of them wouldn't look you in the eye. But by the time they'd finished building that boat, well, each of them was able to stand up and give a little talk to the three hundred people who came to see the launch. That's the real harvest of this place."

BRISTOL MARKS THE divide between forest and field— between cutting trees and growing corn—in this part of

Vermont. Upland, to the east, Addison County tends toward woods broken by occasional opening. West, as the valley levels out toward the lake, more and more of the land is open field, interspersed with woodlots. Brynn and I came out in one of those fields around noontime, a vast expanse of cow corn already higher than our heads. We set off down parallel rows, two feet apart but invisible to each other, and David began talking about how agriculture presents many of the same paradoxes as forestry in this area. There's the same pressure to produce food and timber as cheap commodities, because most customers buy on price. But cheapness always carries a cost. In the forest, it's clearcuts and eroding roads. It's not so different for farmers.

This field, for instance, belongs to one of the county's biggest dairies—they bought the land, ironically, after they made a bundle selling off a parcel near Burlington that became Vermont's first big-box development. On the one hand, they are reasonably conscientious farmers, not spreading their ocean of liquid manure until there is enough spring growth to make sure it won't flow straight into the river. On the other hand, says Brynn, "there used to be fifteen different houses filled with people farming this land. Now it's all one big farm." The cows are confined to a huge barn instead of walking in the fields, standing all day on pavement like city commuters waiting for the bus. The farmers are producing milk at commodity prices, hoping to stay big and efficient enough to compete with the mega-dairies of California and Arizona and Wisconsin, hoping to defy the odds that have shut down 80 percent of Vermont's dairy farmers in the last thirty years. For the hardworking family it might mean a necessary path to survival, but for the region it didn't really replace the smaller-scale farming that had once thrived here. It was, perhaps, a kind of holding action—keeping the land in use, unsubdivided, till an economy emerged that could allow it to be more diversely farmed.

And so, when we finally reached the edge of this sea of corn, emerging on a dirt road, I bade David farewell and set off again to the west—interested to see, among other things, if there were signs of that new economy emerging anywhere. If the same kind of creative thinking he was bringing to forests had begun to bubble up on area farms. If the trend toward bigness was inevitable, or if other visions beckoned.

All morning, walking the back road from Bristol toward Middlebury, I was in open country. There were fields in corn, and meadows and pastures, and there were abandoned fields growing in. An awful lot of former farms had been divided up into house lots—until recently, Vermont law exempted parcels over ten acres from state septic laws, so the houses tended to be spaced about the same distance apart. Many had expanses of grass out front, and for some reason, probably because a thunderstorm was threatening for later in the day, it seemed as if every single man above retirement age was out on his rider-mower. Some had clearly cut their lawns just a day or two before—their passage left no discernible wake, like the Russian babushkas forever brooming their spotless patch of sidewalk. But it was a sign of atavistic devotion nonetheless. Farming may have all but disappeared in this country (fewer than 2 percent of Americans list it as their occupation, making farmers scarcer than prisoners), but some desire to tend the soil persists.

And occasionally it erupts, despite all efforts at suppression. I reached Chris Granstrom's farm about one in the afternoon, and slung my backpack down in his garden shed because the rain was clearly just minutes away now. Granstrom is, come to think of it, tall and skinny, with a broad smile. He arrived in the region twenty-five years ago to attend Middlebury College. "Between my junior and senior year I worked the summer for a dairy farmer a little ways west in Bridport," he says. "As any good farmer should, he did his best to talk me out of staying with agriculture. But I loved the whole thing." And he loved it still, though a little more sadly and wisely. "We've farmed U-pick strawberries here for twenty-one years," he says. "Between that, and my wife teaching, and a little freelance writing, we've made it. On a Saturday in the spring we'll get vast crowds. But you know, we've been growing them in the same soil. Rotating them, of course, but still, by the fourth rotation, they just weren't as vigorous. And I was learning about all this," he says, with a sweep of his hand that took in a small pile of cuttings, his daughter Sara who was busy transplanting them, and a greenhouse beyond. "This" was his new project: wine grapes specially bred for the North, a concept he stumbled across at a website called littlefatwino.com.

ONLY A YEAR after planting, Granstrom now has row upon row of sturdy vines where his strawberries once grew. We're walking them, clipping promising-looking twigs that his daughter—a few weeks from heading off to Middlebury College herself—is transplanting by the greenhouse. "This whole idea of taking cuttings and making them root is kind of magical to me," says Granstrom. "It's sort of astronomical the way it multiplies." Indeed, his business plan relies on that magic—he plans to concentrate on selling nursery stock to others in the area who want to start vineyards of their own.

"Look, the wine will be really nice wine. But probably not world class. So it will be for local supply"—that is, for people who want the pleasure of tasting it not only on their tongues but in their minds as well, who will appreciate the story that comes with it, the same way I cherish the local wood in my house. "There's a huge glut of wine right now in California, New Zealand—that's why you can get Two Buck Chuck or whatever in the supermarket," he says. "But in places like the Finger Lakes in upstate New York, it's worked out better—it's for a local market."

Right about then the thunder finally cracks and the downpour starts, so we retreat back into the shed. Granstrom opens a bottle of the wine he's made from his initial harvest—crisp, like a Riesling, delicious—and he and Sara engage in what is clearly a long-running debate about what to call their winery.

"Lincoln Peak," he says—a peak in the Mount Abe range, clearly visible through the trees.

The New Haven gurgles nearby, now almost flatwater after its tumbling descent from the height of the ridge. "Breadloaf Mountain Winery," I suggest—for the source of the headwaters of the river, and also for its "glass of wine and thou" overtones.

"I just don't know," said Granstrom with a laugh. "My whole life used to involve dealing with words, and now it involves dealing with heavy objects." He looked out through the open doors, where his vines gleamed in the lightening rain. "I have a much more complicated relationship with nature since I became a farmer. Things that seem benign or beautiful when they don't threaten you directly become something else. Like thunderstorms. Or deer. I was out on the tractor the other day and this mother and fawn wandered in—I ended up chasing them around and around the rows in the tractor. Or take the weeds under the grapevines. I talked to a guy not long ago who was going to control the weeds organically—well, they got out of control and now he's using a chainsaw to take out pigweed. So I use Roundup, maybe once a year, in a backpack sprayer. Monsanto is a big, evil, nasty company, but that Roundup starts to degrade as soon as it hits the soil. And what are the alternatives? Well, you could use a mechanical cultivator, but it tears up the vine roots and the soil structure, and it's spewing diesel fuel as it goes. You could do flame weeding, and maybe I will—but that's just driving down the rows with a propane tank. Or I could hire a bunch of migrant workers with hoes. Which is the right answer?"

Just like the woodlot owners trying to figure out how much environmental conscience they can afford, Vermont farmers have to figure out how to stay afloat in an economy where food is treated as a commodity. For many, "organic" agriculture was the salvation—a label that could induce consumers to pay enough more for their dinner that small, local farms stayed viable. Behind the label was a story, just like Lincoln Peak wine will be a story, and VFF wood. "Organic" was "value added" in an almost psychological way, as shoppers looked for some kind of real connection that the shiny rows of supermarket apples, the yellow rafts of "chicken parts," couldn't offer. Organic carried those fuzzy feelings—but now the organic story is being quickly rewritten, as huge growers start to dominate the market. And so, as we shall see, the search is on for the next story that might allow small farmers the margin they need.

Whatever else it turns out to be, that story won't be a fairy tale. "I've watched many intelligent people arrive and try to farm—they're well capitalized and all—and most of them go down in flames," said Granstrom. "And the reason, I finally decided, is that they expect things to go right. You can't think like that. You have to expect things to go wrong. Like, I used to sell apple trees. And when people would come to get them, I'd say, 'You have to watch out for this disease and this scab' and so forth. And they would look at me like 'I'm a virtuous person, my tree's not gonna get that.' But they would, of course. I used to think that way, too—the rain was a blessing on my efforts. But what if it doesn't rain? You're cursed? You can't think like that. You have to replace that kind of thinking with sheer competence."

THE RAIN ENDED, and from Granstrom's farm I crossed Route 7, the two-lane road that is western Vermont's main thoroughfare. (Until last year, all traffic stopped twenty miles south of here every morning and afternoon when a farmer led his herd from the pasture to the milking parlor. The state, with its usual unswerving commitment to speed and efficiency, finally paid to build him a barn on the pasture side, and so one last small reminder of what life once was like disappeared). A little farther west I hit Otter Creek, just above the spot where the New Haven flows in. Despite its diminutive name, Otter Creek is Vermont's longest river; it flows mostly north, rising in the hills around Rutland and eventually pouring into Lake Champlain near Vergennes. Along much of its route it winds through farmers' fields, but this is diverse country—I met Otter Creek just at the top of a rocky whitewater gorge. But instead of exploring that canyon I turned south, walking upstream, through a large forest park that runs right into the county seat of Middlebury.

The thunderstorm had done little to cut the late-afternoon heat, and steam was rising off every puddle. But along the riverbank, giant hemlocks provided their own deep shade, and a spring-loaded carpet of red needles. Peering out through the branches, I watched dragonflies float above the lazy river, and listened to the rising tremolo pulse of insect song, and felt my belly full of wine. Leave Provence to the Provençals, and Tuscany to the Tuscans—the world was altogether sweet enough right here. Why, Provence could kiss my sweaty derriere, I thought, with the slightly sodden pleasure of someone just a trifle drunk. Drunk on that fine Riesling, but even more on the close, humid, singing torpor of an afternoon in the hemlock woods on the edge of Otter Creek. And even more on the sense that life, which in most places seems to me to be spinning apart, was somehow slowly gathering here, deepening, threatening to make sense.

AFTER A COUPLE of miles, the path I was following emerged into Middlebury, shire town and gravitational center of Addison County. It's not a perfect New England village—a sprawling suburban subdivision of cul-de-sacs and split-level ranches bounds the town to the east, and the town fathers carelessly let a short string of McDonald's and Marriott franchises bloom south of town along the highway. But Middlebury still boasts an actual manufacturing district. At the spot where I emerged from the woods, I could see the Cabot Cooperative cheddar plant, the Otter Creek not-so-microbrewery, and half a dozen similar enterprises. And with its downtown, Middlebury hits the New England trifecta: bandstand on the green, towering white Congregational church, and at the far end a college-on-a-hill. In between, past the bank and the bookstore, you cross a bridge over a plunging waterfall on Otter Creek. There's no other bridge for twenty miles to the south, and only a small covered one nearby to the north, so if you're going east to west in this part of the world you pretty much pass through downtown Middlebury. As a result, there's none of that left-out-to-dry-by-the-highway look which afflicts so much of rural America. The college and tourist trade has driven rents high enough that too many of the stores specialize in "gifts," which is to say things that by definition no one actually needs. Still, a Ben Franklin remains, full of venerable merchandise and heavily patronized by my daughter and others of the ten-year-old set who enjoy its penny candy, still priced at a penny. Also a movie theater and a library and an overgrown shoe store that sells underwear and dungarees. Also a fancy restaurant for anniversaries and a smoky bar and a very fine bakery and really what else do you need?

I stood on the bridge in the center of town, watching kids kayaking in the white water beneath the falls, and listening to the passing babel. Most of the year, Middlebury College is a top-tier liberal arts school, as good as any in New England (though just a trifle worried whether Williams and Amherst think of it as often as it thinks of them). In the summer, however, Middlebury gives itself over to a long-running and equally illustrious language school, an operation that has trained generations of diplomats and CIA agents and Peace Corps volunteers by immersing them in the tongue of their choice. These students sign a solemn oath not to utter a syllable of English the whole summer, and as a result much business in town turns into a pantomime of sign language and frustrated pidgin. In a foreign country, you speak the language poorly and the shopkeeper speaks it well; here, you speak the language poorly (at least at first) and the merchant doesn't even know which of the dozen possible tongues you're butchering. The students take it with dire seriousness—one of the ER doctors at the local hospital swears that they have a letter on file from the dean, which they can show to students authorizing them to break their vow and describe their symptoms in the mother tongue.

I wandered on through town, stopping at the small grocery for provisions for the next few days, then at my college office to check my mail. I am a "scholar in residence" at Middlebury, a grand-sounding post that— typical of any job I might attract—carries no actual salary. But it does offer a fine garret, with a view of the Adirondacks, and a speedy computer connection. Better yet, it offers colleagues—Middlebury has built perhaps the finest undergraduate environmental studies department in the nation, and so there's a steady supply of like-minded economists, political scientists, biologists, physicists, theologians, and writers to talk with and learn from. And though I rarely teach, there are students who find their way to my door. Middlebury has its share of handsome and self-satisfied preppies on their way to the important task of investment banking, but it also attracts a steady flow of kids for whom the bucolic setting provides more than backdrop. They start to wonder, à la Chris Granstrom, how they might fit into a place like this. Most of these regular students are gone till the fall, of course, replaced by the worried throng trying to recall how you say "What's on draft?" in Arabic. But a couple of my very favorite students are hanging around for the summer, and I'll get to spend this night with them in perhaps the single most beautiful spot on this calendar-gorgeous campus.

THE MIDDLEBURY COLLEGE Organic Garden lies on a knoll in the middle of a cornfield about a quarter-mile west of the campus. A year ago it was just a bump in that expanse of cow corn. But now—well, to call it a garden is not enough. It's a good half-acre of vegetables, as well-tended and orderly a farmlet as any you'd ever want to see. A new harvest of spinach has just been dispatched to the dining hall for tonight's supper of babel, and doubtless students are even now searching their phrasebooks to find out what they call spinach in Moscow or Madrid. Meanwhile we are sitting around the fire pit, watching our dinner of chard and corn and potatoes steam.

This place was the work of students, right from the start. Like most liberal arts colleges, Middlebury traditionally hasn't shown much interest in agriculture. Any other kind of culture, sure: you can major in film or dance or literature, and rightly so. But colleges developed at least in part to help people escape from the farm, and that old prejudice dies hard. There isn't even a regular course about farming at this college, though it lies in one of New England's most fertile valleys.

A few years ago, though, when Jean Hamilton and

Bennett Konesni were freshmen, they ran into each other in the hallway outside an organic agriculture workshop elsewhere in the state. They agreed, on the spot, that Middlebury needed a student garden. And then, oddly enough, they actually made it happen. (In my days as a wild-eyed student, it was generally accepted that talk was more important than action, but times have changed.) With an ever-growing band of fellow students, they commandeered the college GIS lab, using the computers to overlay maps of soil type with maps of college-owned land; eventually they found the knoll in the cornfield, one of the few nearby outcroppings of rich loam in the valley floor, which is mostly clay best suited for cow corn. They sat down with the guys from dining services, and worked out spreadsheets of what they could sell to the college; then they visited local farmers to make sure they weren't planting crops that would undercut their neighbors' livelihoods. They persuaded the student government to supply cash sufficient for a well and a solar pump; the latter's black photovoltaic panel now rises like a rectilinear sunflower in the middle of the patch. They found seed companies to donate seed, and beekeepers to loan them hives, and before too long the day came to lay down a winter cover crop of rye. And on that afternoon, once the homecoming game was finished, the college president and the chair of the board of trustees both appeared, and spent a happy hour bent over, pulling rocks from the soil. At which point it was very clear it was going to be a success.

A few months after that cover crop went down, and a few months before the first vegetables would be planted, I taught a short course during the college's January term on "Local Food Production." Not because I knew much about it—I have a green mind but a black thumb—but because I was beginning to think that "local" was about to replace "organic" as the key idea in the battle to save small-scale American farming.

For a generation, a certain number of farmers scattered across the country have managed to hang on by growing organic food for consumers willing to pay more for a dinner free of pesticides. That premium was enough to make it possible to survive without the efficiencies of scale that came from vast agribusiness plantations; in Addison County, an organic dairy farmer can get twice as much per hundredweight. Just like David Brynn's family foresters, these family farmers had figured out a way to keep their squash and tomatoes from becoming mere commodities; instead of chemical residue, they came with a residue of story, enough story to justify a living wage. A few years ago, though, the organic movement grew large enough that agribusiness began to pay attention. They started converting a few of their vast fields in the Central Valley or Mexico into "organic farms"—enormous institutions that in every other respect operated like classic corporate giants. It's true that those particular acres were spared the rain of herbicides, but the food grown there still has to be trucked and flown around the world—by some measures, the average leaf of organic produce travels even farther than the 1,500 miles that a bite of conventional food must journey between farm and lip. And once companies like Del Monte started becoming some of the world's biggest organic producers, the premium for a local guy with a couple of acres of really nice organic tomatoes started to shrink. He had no niche left. For two decades, "organic" had meant more than just "pesticide-free"; it also meant "some local guy grew this with his own hands." Now that meaning was evaporating.

But there was a possibility for another story, this one harder to co-opt. If "local" could become the new buzzword, then perhaps it would provide sizzle enough to justify a premium price again, that ten cents more a pound meaning the difference between a farmer making it, and a farm becoming Olde Farm Acres at $49,900 a building lot. That's what Chris Granstrom had been talking about when he noted that Finger Lakes wine was still selling in the Finger Lakes. It's why our local food co-op started posting pictures of the farmers above stacks of their cabbages. And Del Monte simply can't do it—their economies of scale would disappear if customers in Rochester and Eugene and Tampa began demanding food from Rochester and Eugene and Tampa. That's what we studied in our class, anyway—reading Wendell Berry and the other prophets of a new agronomy, and taking field trips to Vermont innovations like The Farmers Diner, a Barre eatery where almost all the ingredients in the hamburgers and milk shakes and french fries are raised within fifty miles of the kitchen door. "Think Locally, Act Neighborly" is their slogan, and so far it seems to be working.

As is usually the case, the best thing about the course was the students, who turned out to be remarkably reflective. I knew from listening to them introduce themselves on day one that six or seven of my twenty-five charges thought they wanted to be small farmers someday. But I wondered if they had actually figured out what that meant—most of these kids were from the same backgrounds of privilege and semi-privilege as the rest of the Middlebury student body. They had the same handsome ease and offhand self-confidence.[1] They were, in other words, made to order for the economy now emerging in our world, and every last one of them could grow up, if they wanted, to make a bundle of money. So one day I asked them to try to figure out how much they thought they'd need to earn a year in order to have the kind of life they wanted. They spent the night figuring, and talked about their results the next day—some said they needed to emulate the suburban lifestyle of their parents in order to feel secure, but for the rest their answers converged in

1. When I first arrived at Middlebury, I wondered where they were hiding the fat, ugly, shy children, imagining some special dorm on the edge of campus. But I never found it.

the neighborhood of $30,000. Which perhaps reflected a certain sweet naïveté—twenty-year-olds don't value insurance quite as highly as do the rest of us—but also a certain deep understanding that I admired. Instead of working to afford certain pleasures, many maintained, they would find their pleasure in their work. Which is a good strategy if you're planning to be a small-scale local farmer.

High on that list of pleasures was food. When I was in college, food and grease were more or less synonymous—a cheese-steak sub was my idea of just fine. I told these students that two of them were to be responsible each day for cooking the rest of us lunch, from whatever local produce they could scrounge in midwinter. Our classroom opened onto a kitchen, and all through the discussion smells would flavor the air. Before long, truly astounding dishes were emerging: leeks gratinée, smoked squash soup, gorgeous frittata. (One fellow took things to their logical extreme, scavenging the January countryside for cattail flour and high-bush cranberries the birds had missed. It tasted . . . local.) A kind of emerging sensual appreciation for this place kept us all in thrall—what would come next? It wasn't like we were in Napa—this was Vermont in January. And yet we ate well, just as people ate well in Vermont for hundreds of years before anyone thought of flying in iceberg lettuce.

And now, out at the garden in midsummer, we were eating like Alice Waters. Walk a few paces and eat a handful of cherry tomatoes; a few paces more and grab a pepper or a peapod, or pull a carrot. Two students from that local-food class were spending the night with me. Chris Howell—tall, skinny, goofy grin—had just finished overseeing construction of a garden shed, framing windows, building a rock patio. The final touch, a sod roof with grass cut from the surrounding knoll—seemed to be taking root. Jean Hamilton, quieter and with a bit of a Mona Lisa smile, had been harder to get to know, but as time had gone on, I'd come to admire her enormously. Partly, I confess, for the pies she'd produced for our class. They looked like pies from the covers of those magazines devoted to high-end country living, and they tasted even better than they looked. But her story interested me even more. The daughter of doctors and the graduate of a top prep school, she was clearly an academic overachiever, like virtually everyone else at Middlebury. But she somehow figured out, early on, that she wasn't going to follow the obvious path. She'd spent one semester of her prep school years at the Mountain School, a working farm in the hills of eastern Vermont where I'd been often, a place where the curricular highlights included lambing, sugar run, spring planting. "That made regular school all the harder," she said—and indeed I think she came to Middlebury more to satisfy her family than herself. More than anyone else, she'd designed the garden now blooming around us. We all three lay back against a sloping berm, drank cool water from an old wine jug

Jean had spiked with a branch of mint, and watched the sky above us—this was the summer when orange Mars came so close.

Even in the dusk I could make out four or five white beehives a few yards away on the edge of the garden knoll. They were, as a curator would say, on loan from the collection of Kirk Webster, one of the most artistic small farmers of the Champlain Valley. He lived a few miles south of my route, so I wouldn't actually get to visit his apiary on my trek. But I'd been thinking of him as I wound my pastoral way through the valley, and one of the lighter burdens in my pack was a photocopy of an article, "The Best Kept Secret," that he'd written a few years before for *Small Farm Journal*. Part memoir, part practical guide, part moral meditation, it told of his long and slow maturation as a beekeeper. "It has been my great privilege, despite having very little to start with and many setbacks, to have started on the path of farming when I was a teenager, to give up doing all other work when I was thirty-seven, and to reach my mid-forties with the prospect of continuing for the remainder of my life," he wrote. "Like a person carrying one tiny candle and trying to find his way in a vast underground cavern, I needed all my faculties to find the right course and put the pieces together into a harmonious whole." Indeed, one of the continuing themes of his essay is the difficulty of learning to farm when the chain of transmission that operated since the start of agriculture has broken down—

when there is no parent to teach you how, or to leave you a working farm. "This state is literally crawling with people bringing their money from elsewhere and investing it in some kind of a 'back to the land' venture. These are some of the nicest and most well-intentioned folk you will meet anywhere . . . but their main contribution has been the very patriotic one deemed essential to democracy by Jefferson and Madison—dispersing the fortunes accumulated by the previous generation so that succeeding generations can rise according to their own wits." In general, he says, these neophytes pick the wrong locations and invest too much capital before they figure out a workable system. By contrast, his own story involved endless trial and error (what to do when tracheal mites plague your bees, or a late spring rains out even the dependable flow of dandelion honey) as he discovered how to propagate queens and nucleus colonies for sale to other beekeepers.

Eventually it all worked. Selling queens, and 30,000 pounds of honey, now netted him 50k a year—that is, half again as much as my enthusiastic students had calculated for their baseline. "After living, and enjoying life, for so long with so little, this frankly seems like an enormous fortune to me," he writes. His only sadness, he wrote, was a certain loneliness. He'd never married, and had no one to pass his carefully collected knowledge on to. "If there are young people any more interested in beekeeping as a way of life, I'd like to have a few of them come here to learn the trade," he wrote at the end of his essay. "I'd like them to get a better start and better grasp of the basics than I did," and if even one or two took up such work as their life's own, "I'd be able at least to approach my own definition of successful beekeeping."

Jean had read Kirk's essay in our class, and he came to our final feast (more pies!). It wasn't many months more before he was teaching her the trick of picking queens from a hive. ("I did fine until the end of the day," she said. "When I started getting tired, I started getting stung.") Soon Jean and Bennett and Kirk and Susannah and Missy and a jumble of other real farmers and would-be farmers and boyfriends and girlfriends were off to visit the organic guru Eliot Coleman at his Maine farm, investigating the possibility of using his novel winter greenhouses in the Champlain Valley. Meanwhile, a local master gardener, Jay Leshinsky, was spending most of his summer in the college garden, offering sage advice; and the dean of the county's organic growers, Will Stevens, was dropping by regularly to look in. (He'd visited our class, too, bringing his account books, which demonstrated the unlikelihood of getting rich in this business, and a pile of his best vegetables, which declared the possibility of prospering nonetheless.) "No one knows better than I do how vulnerable real farming is today," Kirk had written. "But when new farms are spawned, and become associated with the others, some real strength, resilience, and comfort starts to emerge. If we reach the point where communities are farming again, then the flywheel will start to turn on its own, and a movement will emerge that no government or corporation can stop."

Jean and Chris crawled inside the new garden shed to sleep, and I rolled out my tent and lay in it happily. All the wine had long since washed from my system, but I still felt unaccountably happy. To be around young people, who haven't yet made all the compromises and concessions that life will urge them to make, and to see them finding older people who can help them go a different way, is to be reminded that the world really is constantly fresh, and that therefore despair for its prospects is not required.

I PROPPED MY BACKPACK against the trellis of the outdoor patio at downtown Middlebury's Otter Creek Bakery the next morning and gorged myself on sticky buns. Not organic, but sticky. Sated, I strode off to meet Netaka White, who'd agreed to keep me company on the day's saunter.

Netaka is very Vermont—lean, bearded (no ponytail, but it wouldn't look out of place). He was walking slowly today because he was still recovering from a run he'd taken from Vermont to Washington to protest the war in Iraq. "When my wife and I first came to Vermont, we had a craft business," he says. "We were very involved in weaving. And that led to hemp." Ah, hemp. At the confluence of the environmental movement with, say, the drum circle/aromatherapy/crystal movement, hemp has been a hot topic for quite a few years. Did you know that the Declaration of Independence was written on hemp? That Thomas Jefferson grew hemp? That if only we grew hemp now we could save the forests, stop global warming, and have chakra-realigning Tantric orgasms? If not, you might want to visit some of the several million hemp sites on the Web. The week I was writing this chapter, an e-mail arrived from someone who had read one of my books. "You missed the boat on hemp, Bill, in *The End of Nature*. We could have already independicized our nation from OPEC! We could have reversed the Greenhouse Effect, saved the rain forests, fed the Third World. . . . Everything that soy does, hemp does better." Anyway, Netaka had once been a kingpin of hemp. He'd started by weaving the fibers into cloth and sewing the cloth into backpacks and bags. Soon he had a little business going: Artisan Gear. Then the Japanese discovered hemp clothes—discovered them in usual Japanese style, which is to say everybody all at once. Suddenly Netaka had a multimillion-dollar company. Then, just as suddenly, the Japanese moved on to something else—snowboarding clothes, maybe, or fast-food uniforms. Anyway, the company more or less imploded, and Netaka was left with the small retail store he'd started with his wife, Claire, in downtown Middlebury, a place called Greenfields Mercantile. "We made the decision to open it almost overnight—the site became vacant because the previous tenant, a lingerie store, turned out to be doubling as a child-porn download site. They were busted, they tossed their stuff out on the street, and since it was a prime Main Street location, we moved in."

Greenfields Mercantile had specialized, of course, in hemp. When it first opened, thirty manufacturers supplied a wide range of hemp clothing, hemp accessories, even hemp vinaigrette. But the supply steadily shrank— federal agents cracked down on one manufacturer after another. "The feds have taken the position that all cannabis is bad cannabis. The stuff we use is incredibly low in THC. The industry has standards to make sure that hemp oil is THC-free, but it doesn't matter. It's all politics." Anyway, Middlebury couldn't really support an eco-fashion store, so they branched out, adding a coffee-house and café.

Still, old dreams die hard. As we wandered toward the northern border of town, past the covered bridge, past open meadows and woodlots, Netaka said, "There's no reason we shouldn't be walking by fields of hemp right here. The University of Vermont did a study, it showed that Addison County was the very best place for this stuff in the whole state, all the right soil types. Heck, there's still feral hemp growing in Addison County from before the legislative ban in the 1930s." A few paces farther and he said with a resigned sigh, "Do you know they're building houses with hemp in Canada? It's fantastic insulation—

high R-value, very breathable, completely sustainable." There's something sweet and noble and for the moment utterly quixotic about this particular quest, so Netaka continues to branch out. He's taken out some of the shelves of slow-moving hemp shampoos—more and more his store is specializing in free-trade coffee and in soups made from local ingredients. Before we'd gone more than a few lots farther down the road, in fact, he'd pulled himself out of the dumps, his entrepreneurial gene had reasserted itself, and he was imagining a sign in the window keeping track of what percentage of that day's food came from Addison County. "There's a bakery in Crown Point—all they use is organic Champlain Valley wheat and they're doing great," he said. "I bet we could do that. Local really could be the new organic!"

Two things interrupted our reverie before it could really take off. One was a hawk, perched out at the end of a big pine branch by the side of the road; it screeched several times, and then began to fly in looping dips, back and forth over us, time and again. The second was a driveway that led to the University of Vermont's Morgan Horse Farm. Now, we'd each driven past this big barn dozens of times, and we knew that it drew tourists from around the Northeast, but of course neither of us had ever gone, any more than New Yorkers visit the Statue of Liberty. When you're on vacation you have time to take in sights, but when you're at home you drive by them on the way to somewhere else, somewhere you're supposed to get. On foot, though, there's no reason not to stop. So we paid our five dollars, shucked our packs, and joined the tour guide, who was just beginning her spiel.

Justin Morgan, it turned out, was a local music teacher who lived in Vermont in the years following the Revolution. Someone in Massachusetts owed him a debt, and though he'd been counting on cash, Morgan was forced to take his payment in the form of a small bay colt. He started walking him home, hoping someone would buy him along the way, but the horse was smaller than the draft animals settlers were using to clear New England's fields. As it happened, Morgan was lucky: his horse turned out to be something of a miracle, able to outrace and outpull every other horse in the neighborhood. "And he was a great breeding stallion," the guide said. "We understand now that he was a genetic mutant with dominant genes, something that hasn't happened before or since. He always bred true. By the time he died at the age of thirty-two, he'd sired enough foals to establish a breed. The Morgan horse has a beautiful crested neck, and a compact body frame with a sense of refinement. They've been used for everything from cavalry horses to family horses." (Frost has a gorgeous poem, "The Runaway," about a Morgan colt leery of his first snowfall.) Still, the breed was about to die out in the late nineteenth century when Addison County's great benefactor, Joseph Battell, built this beautiful farm to save it from extinction. Now owned by the university, it houses sixty to eighty horses, and breeds twenty new foals a year. Apprentices bustled everywhere—young women, who compete for the chance to put in fifty- and sixty-hour weeks, were training horses on a lunge line, currying horses, leading horses to the "breeding phantom," which functions as a kind of equine inflatable love doll for efficient semen collection. Demand is high for the steeds, who are truly handsome in their muscled sleekness—raffle tickets for a chance at one of this year's foals were going fast.

All of which was enough to get us talking again as we walked away. Here was a story about some agricultural innovation that appeared pretty much from nowhere and, with the right nurturance, *took*. Hemp hasn't taken yet—and won't, until we come to grips with our drug hysteria. But hey, there are other possibilities. "I'm helping coordinate a local group that's looking into biodiesel," Netaka said. "You can run a car on soybean oil, on rapeseed. Or you can use one hundred percent vegetable oil, or create blends with petroleum, stretching the supply and lowering emissions. We'd like to have a local bio-refinery—and a pump right in Middlebury, with Addison County–grown gas." I felt him growing more alive, energetic. "You can use it for home heating oil, you know—a fuel one hundred percent locally derived. Even the ferries crossing the lake could run on it!" On we strode, arms swinging.

This is what Vermont is like right now—a lot of fascinating dreams, some of them fever dreams, about how this place might be successfully inhabited. Wine grapes, sweat-equity community forests, college gardens with solar pumps, high-tech wood energy, diners serving local ham and eggs, community slaughterhouses. Ferries running on local biodiesel! Every one of them is an attempt to interfere with history, which at the moment looks as though it should go this way: dairy farms fail or consolidate; farmland turns into second homes or retirement homes or just home-homes, as Burlington sprawls south and north. Interfering with history is hard, because its momentum is so strong: the march of the big box stores, the decline in the number of farmers, the demographic tides of our population. But sometimes that history churns up its own countercurrents. If the future seems unlikely to answer enough yearnings, then people will look for exits.

The last time that happened, of course, was the 1960s and early 1970s—which was also the last moment when there were as many dreams across this landscape. Like northern California, rural Vermont was one of the places that drew yearning counterculturalists. Don Mitchell, whose farm I was now wearily approaching, was perhaps the single perfect specimen. Born in Chicago in 1947, he'd made it to Swarthmore College by the time the sixties were in full swing. From there, with his girlfriend Cheryl, he'd hitchhiked around the country, including Big Sur, Carmel, San Francisco. At twenty-two, based on his experiences, he wrote his first novel, with the

Ur-title *Thumb Tripping*. It was an instant hit—"a pilgrimage to nowhere that slices neatly across the current scene," the *New York Times* declared—and Mitchell was hired to write the screenplay. Directed by a twenty-three-year-old, it co-starred Michael Burns and Meg Foster as what *TV Guide* called "two happy-go-lucky flower children," not to mention Bruce Dern as one of many creeps the pair encounter on their hitchhike through paradise. By the end, said one reviewer, "with the audience numb from the ghastly parade of subhumanity lurking out there, the two youngsters tire of each other and go their separate ways."

In real life, however, Don and Cheryl stayed together. With the money they made from the movie, they bought a Porsche and then they bought this farm in the central valley town of New Haven. It's a spread of undulating meadow set against the rocky outcrops of a low mountain, one of the most thoroughly Vermont settings imaginable. They had their share of adjustment problems—one of the funniest stories I've ever heard was his description of coming out one morning to find the cows licking the chrome off his sports car—but unlike so many of their peers, they stuck. Stuck to a place, stuck to each other, built a life. And slowly changed. When their children began to arrive, they took up farming with real seriousness: "Caring for livestock and making hay and managing a large garden became a wonderful project to bond our family together with a sense of shared purpose," he says.

He raised lambs, in part because the land was suited to them—at its height around the Civil War, Vermont, where grass grows easily, had been sheep pasture to the world. But the business had gone into terminal decline once competition from big Western ranches, and then Australia and New Zealand, caused the price to plummet. (At the moment you can't clear enough selling wool to pay the shearer.) But Mitchell did find one market: Easter lambs for the ethnic market in the big city. It meant breeding his ewes with one eye on the Greek Orthodox liturgical calendar, so that he could time his slaughter for the right week. And it wasn't exactly a living—he kept writing, especially essays about the country life for *Yankee* magazine and the *Boston Globe.* "When I think of all the inappropriate talents, the varieties of ignorance and wealth of misinformation," he wrote in one collection of those pieces, "I am filled with laughter and amazement. Imagine people like me helping to create a new agricultural industry." But he was indisputably a farmer. And there were, indisputably, 260 sheep in the pasture this night, softly baaing.

During thirty years of caring for those flocks, Mitchell developed a certain allergy to romanticism. The week I wandered through, he was making final changes to the galleys of his first novel in two decades, *The Nature Notebooks,* which could almost be described as antienvironmentalist. It tells the story of a handsome and charismatic eco-warrior who arrives in Vermont from parts west, seduces three local women, and manages to employ them all in his scheme to sabotage the transmission towers and ski lifts atop Mount Mansfield. Told through the journals of the three women, it offers Mitchell a chance to lampoon the excesses of modern nature writing, "a jug of milk in which very little cream has risen to the top—because very little cream is present. . . . I'm particularly annoyed," he writes, "by a histrionic strain within this genre that tends to be self-absorbed, self-congratulatory, and vaguely autoerotic. Its modern practitioners strike me as exploiting nature for their own selfish purposes, just as surely (although admittedly more benignly) as loggers, miners, whalers, and oil drillers." You could say he's become a mild curmudgeon, or a modern version of the slightly cranky Yankee farmer: "I happen to dislike what I take to be a preachy and self-righteous strain among environmentalists who wear their values on their sleeves," he says. "Environmentalists will have a better chance of succeeding when people adopt its perspectives simply because they make practical sense." It seems unwise to raise the prospect of hemp, or even biodiesel, although I do mention Chris Granstrom's fine new wine as we eat dinner with his extended family out by the pond.

On the other hand, his daughter Anais is there for dinner, freed for the weekend from Arabic summer school and its sacred language pledge. And she is as open and confident as he must have been in his college days. She's a singer/songwriter—a really good singer/songwriter, who draws big crowds whenever she plays on campus, who was named a top young artist at last year's New Folk competition in Texas. Her voice is gorgeous, but it's tough, too, and her lyrics can scratch—she plays me the tapes of a concert she gave last spring at the college, the culmination of an independent study on protest music of the sixties. It includes a tune about, maybe, the Iraq war—"Did we know, in our house on fire with all we own, what it is that makes a house a home? In the end, did we watch it all on CNN, what it is to be American?" She's powerful, and she may have a real career ahead of her, and it's fun to sit and talk about how to escape the monoculture of the music business, which is as deadly in its way as the monoculture of the Farm Belt. Maybe local music is the way. Maybe if everyone's downloading everything for free off the Net, musicians will go back to earning their keep the way musicians have done since Homer—by sharing their songs live with their neighbors. Maybe all of us in Addison County will be drinking Lincoln Peak wine and listening to Anais in ten years—maybe she'll be our bard.

Lying in Mitchell's field that night, listening to the occasional bleat from the flock, I keep looking for the eyes of the mountain lion he swears he saw not long ago in this very spot. (Mountain lions are one of the recurring phantoms of this part of the world, and I've always yearned to see one; since Don has two sturdy guard dogs, predators don't worry him much.) Finally I drift off, only to be awakened near dawn by the suddenly more excited baas from the other side of the pond. Don and Cheryl have come out to move the light electric fence that keeps the flock confined to an acre or two a day, and with the prospect of fresh new grass suddenly close at hand, the sheep were discovering an urgent hunger. (The easily rolled wire fences are a brilliant innovation, allowing pasture to rejuvenate constantly by making daily rotation simple work.) I hustled over to lend a hand, just for the pleasure of seeing the animals go charging into their new, uneaten acre, diving in with real brio to the new green stems. I ate my cereal with gusto, too, and packed. Don, who'd built six of the eight structures on the farm, was already on the roof of the new addition he was finishing, pounding nails before the sun got too high. I said my good-byes and strode off, to the west again.

My day's walk would carry me to the shore of Lake Champlain and the very edge of Vermont, but first it would take me through the absolute heart of the state's agricultural belt, the flat fine farmland of New Haven and Waltham and Panton. The map offered plenty of back roads to choose from, long, straight, unpaved lanes built to make sure that farmers could get their crops to market. The day started hot, but with just enough overcast to take the edge off the sun. And so, for a few hours, I was in my own miniature Midwest, walking corn-lined gravel roads, able to see pickups coming three miles away by the plume of dust that rose in their wake. This land still looks prosperous, for the decline of Vermont agriculture that began with the marginal soils and chilly summers on the steep hill farms 2,000 feet higher up hasn't yet devastated these prime lands, which are warmed in the winter by the nearby lake. Even so, however, they're not in California, and the usually dropping price of fluid milk presses on them from one side. And the ever-growing price of land for second homes presses from the other, for these farms could easily be subdivided into twenty building lots, each with a spectacular view of the Adirondacks. These farms exist in a kind of (extremely hardworking) limbo, waiting to see if some new possibility of the type I've been describing—a local-food movement, a biodiesel market—will actually appear, or if they're fated for the same end as so many others.

For the moment, though, they're timeless—you can't tell from a look across the landscape which decade you are in. At first it seemed quiet to me, with just the occasional bark of a dog to break the silence. Before long, though, I'd quieted down enough myself to notice that it was a noisy kind of silence. The pulsating hum of insect warble rose and fell in murmuring waves across the landscape, growing louder near wet spots but never subsiding. I don't still myself to hear it often enough, but it's on my own short *Billboard* chart of favorite sounds, right up there with Tumbling Brook, Wind in Pines, and (wooden) Bat on Ball. It's an almost geological sound, the same, I imagine, for the millions of summers ever since those scraping wings and legs evolved. It's pure life, just asserting its existence, announcing the triumphant biology of our sweet planet. It's the sound we will all subside into someday, life on automatic.

I ATE MY LUNCH in a little copse of trees and wandered on, lulled by the sound and the heat and the long, straight lines until finally I came to something new: a watery slough, Dead Creek, that stretches ten miles north to south across this section of the valley. If the shore of Lake Champlain represents the physical boundary of Vermont, in a sense this line of slow-moving water a couple of miles to its east represents the conceptual one—the place where questions of nature began to loom as large as questions of agriculture, economy, and sociology. There was a long way yet to go before I reached the heart of the big Adirondack wilderness, but those mountains were starting to loom in my mind—the questions that wilderness raises were present in miniature here. Also present, and full-sized, was Warren King, the perfect person with whom to start thinking them through.

Warren actually lives up in Ripton, a few minutes' bushwhack through the woods from my house. He and his wife, Barry, are the sort of people who make a place tick—there's not a civic good work in which they're not implicated. But it's conservation in particular that moves them, and for Warren, it's birds. He studied ornithology at Cornell, and his life list includes pretty much everything save the passenger pigeon (and the ivory-billed woodpecker—but he was in Cuba winter before last, just in case). Dead Creek is one of his most frequent haunts, because the northern end of it is managed as a wildlife refuge, and in recent years it has begun to draw great quantities of birds—in particular, flocks of snow geese numbering 25,000 or more arrive each October, jetting around the valley in their tight Vs, and settling in on a few fields that line the state two-lane. "It's the premier wildlife spectacle in the state—sometimes there are a hundred cars parked along the roadside watching," Warren says; he's been known to set up his spotting scope and stand there all day so that others could take a gander at the geese. "Overall, Dead Creek is a pretty significant bird hotspot," he continues. "The fields are planted to some kind of goose food, like buckwheat or corn, and then they're instructed to do a careless job harvesting so there are plenty of kernels left on the ground. The fields are off limits to hunters, but the marsh is extensive and in good shape. It was designed as a waterfowl refuge, so hunting is encouraged"—indeed, near the main goose flyway the reeds are filled with blinds where hunters sit all afternoon, waiting for a careless bird. "But the birds very quickly get a knowledge of how far the guns can fire," he says.

So we might begin the muddle this way: Vermont's

premier wildlife spectacle comes about because managers plant fields in order to lure geese so that hunters can shoot them. Which might strike an environmentalist as a little crazy, except that without the hunters the snow geese might not be here. On the other hand, we've created such fine goose havens in the lower forty-eight that their numbers have exploded, and so when they return to the Arctic to breed they do massive damage, tearing up sedge grass by its roots and destroying the tundra. So maybe more hunting is the sane response. Or maybe not.

If we're going to talk about wildness, and believe me we are, we have to face the truth that it's a little hard to separate out the natural and the artificial, a little hard to figure out exactly where we're planting our feet. For instance: this afternoon Warren and I are standing on a little bridge above Dead Creek a few miles south of the waterfowl refuge. "You notice how the water is kind of mocha here?" he asks. "One reason is the clay soils—the particles can stay in suspension almost forever. And those particles get stirred up all the way along the creek by carp fanning their tails." But carp are an exotic species, introduced from afar. So is the mocha color "right"?

A walk with Warren is an ambling, happy disquisition, interrupted frequently by sightings of one thing or another, often things with wings. "There's a black-crowned night heron," he'll say. "At this point we don't know where in Vermont they nest. Isn't it nice to have some pieces of information still out there to discover?"

Or, "Look, there's a yellow warbler. As bright as any taxicab you'll ever see, but with brown and red streaks on the chest." Or, "Oh my, there's a red-spotted purple. That's a white admiral subspecies. Butterflies are kind of a new thing for me."

But over and over we kept returning to the same kind of philosophical conundrums. It wasn't just carp: Dead Creek was also host to a variety of other exotic and invasive species. "Ooh, water chestnut," said Warren. "We've gotten rid of that on the Lemon Fair River [that is, Warren and Barry spent weeks pulling the plants up by the roots], but there's still a little population over here in Dead Creek. The nut is an extraordinarily vicious-looking thing, like a caltrop. It gets stuck on the plumage and feet webbing of geese and ducks, and they carry it from one body of water to the next." The scrubby meadows and hedgerows around Dead Creek were also filled with plants that, strictly speaking, Shouldn't Be There. Honeysuckle. Wild parsnip. "Oh, there's an interesting battle going on here. This is a Eurasian buckthorn, an invasive species. And this is a gray dogwood, which is supposed to be here. Over here the buckthorn has ascendancy, but here the dogwood is still king."

So do you wring your hands over this, rooting for the dogwood and the prickly ash, rooting up the buckthorn? Or do you just decide that nature is whatever it is—that since the world is in constant flux, there's no real damage that can be done to it? For instance, Warren pointed out a small elm tree. "As you know, they get Dutch elm disease when they're about twenty. But they start producing seed when they're ten. So they have a decade before the fungus starts to shut them down. As a result, we're getting increasing numbers of elm trees that get to be about that big. Not the big umbrella street-lining trees we grew up with. But they have this niche now. They're an understory tree—that's just what they are now." Are we to mourn the passing of big elms? Celebrate the success of this fungus we helped introduce? Merely marvel at all the different stratagems that evolution puts in play?

And the questions get more complicated than that, even. A few hundred yards west of the creek, we wandered out into a big hayfield. "Grassland is an interesting subject in this part of the world," Warren said. "There are a small number of species—bobolink, upland sandpiper, eastern meadowlark, grasshopper sparrow, savanna sparrow, Henslow's sparrow—that require it. They make their nests in the tall grass." But in recent years, as farms have been abandoned, much of that grassland has grown into scrub forest. And the grass that's left has become more intensively managed, with farmers trying to get an extra cut of hay—which means harvesting prior to mid-July, before the birds can get their broods safely off. "So the question is, do you manage for them, or do you let nature take its course?" That is, do you set aside some fields to maintain in grass, cutting them even though no one is farming, and cutting them late so that the birds have time to nest? Or do you let nature and the economy take its course? "Henslow's sparrow is already gone from the state, the grasshopper sparrow is down to a few pairs in the state. Bobolinks aren't at any great risk yet, but that's the general tendency." Maybe that's bad, and maybe that's "right." I mean, the only reason those birds were here in the first place is that farmers came in and opened up the woods. Or maybe not—maybe they were opened up first by the Indians who lived in this valley. Are Indians different—more "natural"—than the rest of us humans, and does that change our relationship to the bobolink? Maybe our attachment to grasshopper sparrows is only sentimental, romantic.

These questions of what constitutes the natural, what composes the real, when you draw the baseline, how much change a place can stand before it loses its essence— they are the questions that will grow stronger and louder the farther west we go, into the Adirondack wild (whatever "wild" means). For now, it's enough perhaps to note what Warren and Barry King have done: they've pulled up the water chestnut and the purple loosestrife, because those exotics were overrunning everything in their path and decimating the food supply for a wide variety of animals. They have not fished every carp out of Dead Creek, or cut down every buckthorn. When the snow geese come through in the fall, they stand by the roadside with their spotting scope so neophytes can take a look. Once a year, under the auspices of the local Audubon chapter, they organize Dead Creek Wildlife Days—which features plenty of birdwatching, but also hunters showing off the retrieving skills of their bird dogs. That is to say, they do what they can, guided by a certain tropism toward "the natural" but governed by common sense and a dose of wry humility.

Mostly they make sure to marvel. "Do you hear the flicker calling just now?" asks Warren—I hadn't, of course, but now I did. "Oh look, that's a harrier. The white rump patch, the wings held at a slight dihedral. Now this, this is a native—it's prickly ash. It's a tough customer. Get in a thicket of that, and you're going to give blood. And speaking of thorns, look over here. This is a hawthorn. Look at the size of that thorn. You know who likes hawthorns? A bird called a shrike. It looks like a mockingbird, but it's a predator. They catch smaller birds, they bring them to a spine like this, and they hang them up on it just like a local butcher would hang up a side of beef." That's nature, or something like it.

WARREN TURNED BACK to the east finally, and I kept on my trudge, near enough now to the big lake that I could catch glimpses of it through the fields. The closer I got, the bigger the houses became, as if in observance of some iron law of real estate. Finally, down right on the lakeshore, the most oversized manse of all sat on a sloping lawn, every tree cleared for hundreds of yards. After all the quieter places I'd been in the last week—Don Mitchell's tucked-in farm, the lovely knoll of the college garden, John Elder's sugarbush—this place looked naked, bald, without a trace of modesty. Two big signs on the driveway announced the obvious, that the road was "private," that wanderers on foot could find some other way to reach the lake. Two golf holes were cut into the lawn, little flags hanging limp in the hot afternoon. This place was by any definition an invasive, a blight or a fungus spread by money pouring in from the south. The kind of place that suppressed natural life, community life, just as thoroughly as the water chestnut in the creek.

But again I held the sermon back, calmed a little by the lessons on flux and resiliency that Warren had been teaching, and calmed, too, that I knew another route down to the shore of Champlain. Before half an hour had passed, my feet were in the cool water, in a little bay under a limestone bluff covered with cedar and oak. I'd come to the edge of Vermont, and New York beckoned across the water. Or, as I'd started to think, I'd come to the middle of this watershed, this cultureshed.

IN THE MIDDLE distance a big aluminum rowboat came steadily across the lake. As it grew nearer I could make out the oarsman—a small man, shirt off, as wiry and muscled as a statue. Tanned and smiling, he looked like a photo from a muscle magazine before steroids turned physiques grotesque.

I'd planned the route and timing of my trek in part because I wanted to cross Lake Champlain with John Davis, whom I'd known for half his life and half mine. We'd met first in Tucson, Arizona—well, this is going to require more explaining.

I hadn't always been particularly interested in the outdoors. I went from college straight to *The New Yorker,* where I was the steadiest writer for the Talk of the Town section, about as urban a job as it's possible to imagine. But in my mid-twenties—in the mid-1980s—two things happened. One was that I started to work on my first long piece of writing, an account for *The New Yorker* about where every pipe and wire in my Manhattan apartment came from and went. I followed the water pipes to the Catskill reservoirs, and traveled to Hudson Bay to see the enormous dams producing power for Con Ed, and spent days on New York harbor with the giant garbage barges—and along the way had the sudden insight that the physical world *actually mattered*. That this came as an insight says much about how I—and perhaps most good suburban Americans—had grown up. But suffice it to say that all of a sudden things that had always seemed like scenery and props for the great drama of ideas and money and politics now seemed much more central to me: air, I'm talking about, and water, and oil.

At the same time, by a fluke, I came to the Adirondacks for a winter—to the writers' colony at Blue Mountain Lake, where I actually wrote the piece about my apartment. I spent that winter falling in love with these woods, which would transform my life. And one day, in the bathroom at Blue Mountain, I came across a copy of the *Earth First! Journal,* which would help transform my sense of the world.

Earth First! was still young in those days, a radical environmental group that rose in the Southwest desert in the time of James Watt and Ronald Reagan. Less a group, really, than a style: cantankerous, uncompromising, convinced that the fire had gone out of the wilderness movement and that it was their duty to reignite it. Founded by a few friends, Earth First! drew its inspiration from the pages of the great desert writer Edward Abbey, and in particular his novel *The Monkey Wrench Gang,* an account of a small redneck band that crosses the desert blowing up coal mines and highway bridges in defense of the wild. Earth First! was launched in an illegal ceremony atop Glen Canyon Dam, the concrete plug that had flooded deep, gorgeous canyons of the Colorado into Lake Powell (Lake Foul, to Abbey). The small band gathered atop the dam and unrolled a massive plastic crack down its face, symbolizing their hope that it would soon disappear. These guys (and they were almost all guys) fascinated me—their frank and joyful denial that humans mattered most (*Earth* First!), their pugnacity at a moment when Reagan and the Right were rolling over every more responsible advocate of a normal, balanced America, their willingness to tip over every sacred cow, even the environmental ones (Abbey would, proudly, toss beer cans out the car window as he finished them, arguing that if the government was going to graze and mine the land into oblivion, worrying about litter was sentimental camouflage, especially along those linear landfills called roads). And so I set out to investigate, traveling to Utah to hike with Abbey, and to Idaho for a hard-drinking week in the glorious Challis National Forest at the group's annual encampment. And to headquarters, such as it was, in the Tucson home of founder Dave Foreman. Outside, it was a normal Southwestern ranch-style home in a cul-de-sac kind of neighborhood. Inside, it was marvelous chaos—people bunking here and there, planning one mysterious action or another, maps of wilderness areas on every wall, phones ringing constantly in the way they used to—*ringing,* not playing the first measure of some pop hit.

The one calm human being in the middle of all that storm was also the youngest, the most clean-cut, and by far the healthiest looking. John Davis was the editor of the *Earth First! Journal,* which was the glue that held the anarchic group more or less together. I watched him paste up a few stories—a blockade of a road into some planned clearcut on an Oregon national forest, an early tree-sit by some protesters in redwood country. Every half hour or so he would rise from his desk, walk over to the doorjamb, and do twenty or thirty pull-ups. Refreshed, he'd get back to his labors. The journal he was editing reflected the group's prevailing ethos: new editions were published not in accord with the conventional months, but with the pagan calendar (Beltane, Samhain); the lively letters column was called "Dear Shit-fer-Brains"; and the most-read column was doubtless "Dear Ned Ludd," where readers would write in with questions about, say, what type of sugar to pour down a bulldozer's gas tank if you wanted to disable it. It was, in other words, thoroughly irresponsible. Except that in a world where the rise of radical conservatism still seemed fresh in its craziness, this response also seemed thoroughly necessary. As if someone was actually giving as good as we were getting. And I was twenty-five at the time—it seemed deeply romantic, this idea of wilderness as the ultimate good.

In retrospect, I realize I saw Earth First! near the end of its glory days. Two things happened. One, as with all cool scenes, it was soon inundated—since it was the only fighting game in town, activists from a dozen other causes descended, most of them more hippie than redneck. "They weren't all that much concerned with wilderness," Davis recalled as he rowed, steady and powerful, across the lake. "The last straw may have come at one of the annual rendezvous, when one of the newcomers stood up and demanded that Earth First! get involved in rent control." Two, the FBI arrived. In our post-9/11 world, it seems hard to believe that the Feds left the group alone as long as they did: they were, after all, advocating a dozen creative varieties of sabotage. But it wasn't until fairly late in the game that they swooped down, arresting Foreman and charging him with instigating a scheme to tear down a bunch of power lines in the Arizona desert. In truth, the charge was nonsense—the trial, when it finally happened, featured a government informer so drug-addled that the prosecutors had to argue that LSD didn't interfere with his ability to be a cogent witness. But that was much later.

"I'd been traveling when the arrests happened, and friends and colleagues back in Tucson said not to come back," remembers Davis. "So I spent most of that summer traveling in the East. Not on the run, but keeping a low profile." Within a few months it was clear that things would not return to normal. And so the movement began to split apart. The hippie wing kept some of the old spirit alive, still publishing the *Journal,* still marking the pagan holidays. But Foreman, Davis, and a good many others were a little tired of the bravado, and no longer convinced direct action would deliver much except police harassment. They split off to start a new, very different, journal, this one called *Wild Earth*. Now a decade old, it's become the intellectual center of a new movement for wilderness, working with some of the country's leading conservation biologists to draw detailed maps and plans for the eventual rewilding of big chunks of the planet. But at the beginning, the most interesting question was where it would be located.

In the United States, heads have always turned west when we've thought about nature. Our vocabulary and grammar of wilderness came most of all from John Muir's summer in the Sierra; our picture of the wild came through the lens of Ansel Adams, traveling the mountains and deserts of California and Nevada. Yellowstone, Yosemite, Alaska, the Rockies—those are the icons. And for Earth First!, too, it had always been the vast Western wildlands—the Gila Wilderness of New Mexico, the Bob Marshall Wilderness of Montana, the Siskiyous of Oregon, all home to wolves or grizzlies or rattlesnakes, giant firs, ancient bristlecone pines, the charismatic flora and fauna of wild America.

But John Davis had grown up in New Hampshire. "I'd been in Tucson five years. I was starting to really miss fresh water," he says. "I have the Eastern forest in my bones. I can be away for a little while, but then I start to pine for it." Not only that, he had a point to make: "that wilderness was not just a Western thing." And so he turned eastward, and in so doing turned, almost inevitably, to the Adirondacks, the biggest and wildest patch of land this side of the Mississippi. "I knew about the Adirondacks because I'd read an article in *National Wildlife* magazine," he says. "My grandmother gave me *Ranger Rick,* and then, when I was a little older, *National Wildlife.* Anyway, I was in sixth grade and I read about the Adirondacks and I was amazed by it. Very taken by it. I knew I wanted to go there someday." His first trip, however, was less than idyllic. It was shortly after he'd left Tucson, and he was with a friend. "It was hot, muggy. We stopped somewhere to camp, and it was completely miserable. Tom managed to get a solo tent up amid the blackflies. I stayed in the cab of the truck. With the windows closed, it was too hot. If I opened them the bugs were impossible. I finally got up at 4:00 a.m. to go for a very fast walk."

"Once I really started exploring the Adirondacks, though, I knew I wanted it to be my home region," he said. "There really was no place else."

By now we were almost completely across the lake, pulling into a small cove in the woods. Looking back at the Vermont shore, we could see dozens of those big second-home mansions, mile after mile of development. On the New York coast, however, the woods run almost unbroken down to the water's edge; much of the land we were approaching south of Split Rock Point is state-owned, "forever wild" under Article 14 of the state's constitution. The Adirondacks aren't *all* wild—within the 6-million acre Adirondack Park, only 3 million acres are protected public land; the other 3 million are in private hands. Most of that is timberland, but there are also small towns scattered throughout, and ever more vacation homes. Still, that 6 million acres makes it roughly the same size as Vermont, only with 140,000 people instead of 700,000. It makes Vermont—statistically America's most rural state—seem densely populated. It is not, as I have said, pure wilderness, any more than Vermont is purely settled. But it tends toward wildness. And one of John's missions is to make it wilder yet.

We landed the rowboat and struck off through the woods, first on a path and then on a track and then just cross-lots through the puckerbrush. The afternoon was steamy, and within minutes a cloud of mosquitoes descended. By dint of topography, and because so much of the Adirondacks have never been tilled and drained, the region seems infinitely wetter than Vermont. No placid agricultural rivers like Otter Creek, but ten thousand little streams backed up into a million beaver pools. The cartographers claim three thousand lakes for the park, but it all depends on definition—if you're a mosquito, the number of places to call home is many orders of magnitude higher. I slathered on some toxic DEET, John a bit of organic repellent, and we continued toward his house. And he continued to tell his story.

"When we started *Wild Earth,* I was actually getting a salary. Not much, but I was saving every penny. And I knew I wanted to buy land. All those years of reporting and editing bad news—I wanted the satisfaction of seeing a place saved." His father actually found the parcel, forty-five acres with a listing log cabin. "As soon as I saw it, I thought immediately: 'This is the place.' Hemlock Rock Wildlife Sanctuary, I started calling it. One of the first things I did was to climb a big white pine—to the west I could see Coon Mountain and nothing but forest. I looked on the map and, sure enough, that area was protected in part by the Nature Conservancy. And to the other side was Split Rock Wild Forest, 4,000 acres of state land. We were right in the middle."

Anywhere else in the east, it would have seemed wild indeed. But in fact the Champlain Valley is the least protected part of the Adirondacks; the few miles between the lake and the start of the high mountains were traditionally farmed, and the state acquired much less land there than in the more rugged uplands. "Conservationists have tended to see the Champlain Valley as a buffer," Davis said. "But there's important wildlife habitat here. People think of it as bucolic—from Willsboro to Port Henry it looks a lot like Vermont, and people love that, don't want it to change. Environmentalists have generally assumed their job here is to maintain that bucolic landscape. Which is fine, but it's not enough. You can't completely consign the valleys to human dominance. That's the western model—wilderness in the rocks and ice, people everywhere else." So John quickly had a second job: trying to build a truly intact corridor connecting the lake with the High Peaks.

John's friend Tom Butler—who eventually succeeded him as editor at *Wild Earth*—met us a few miles on, and together we all climbed Coon Mountain, a rocky little knob smack in the middle of the proposed corridor. The view from the top showed plenty of little squares of hay meadow, but it also showed the obvious forest connection they were trying to enlarge and protect. "You get up here and you ask yourself: 'If I'm a bear, how do I get from the lake to the mountains,' " Tom said. "From up here, too, you can see what a dramatic place this is. The elevational gradient is astounding—the lowest place on the continent is the bottom of Lake Champlain, which is 300 feet below sea level just off Split Rock. From there it's just a few miles to the top of Giant Mountain, which is 4,600 feet."

"We have this opportunity at Split Rock partly because of geological accident," adds John. "There's a band of bedrock underlying the High Peaks that extends through to the lake right here. It's much more rugged, cliffier, ledgier than the rest of the valley, and so it was less farmed. At one time or another, any given point was probably cleared for sheep pasture, but usually they gave up. Because of that challenging geology, we have this possibility for a corridor."

BECAUSE OF THAT challenging geology, and because of another accident, too. After a few years, John left *Wild Earth* to take a job with the Foundation for Deep Ecology, promoting "wildlands philanthropy." Which is to say, rich people buying tracts of land in order to conserve them. (The prototype, and John's mentor, is Doug

Tompkins, who purchased a huge slice of Chile and has recently bitten off a chunk of Argentina.) At a conference he helped organize on the subject in Boston, John met Jamie Phillips, a Manhattan fashion photographer whose stepfather had made a small fortune, set up a foundation, and then died. "Jamie ran the show at the Eddy Foundation, and he could have gone in any number of directions. But he told me he wanted to be able to walk a piece of land he had saved." Within a few weeks John had him up in a small airplane flying over the proposed Split Rock Wildway; within a few weeks after that he'd bought his first parcel, 535 acres on the Boquet mountains. "And after that he really had land-buying in his blood," says John. So far the foundation has acquired about 2,000 acres of the 10,000 they someday hope to protect.

Phillips relocated to a small house in the middle of the property, its walls lined not with his photos but with maps full of pins marking possible land sales. I pulled off my pack in his yard, happy for the rest. Overjoyed, in fact, when he proposed a *drive* around the area so he could show off some of their acquisitions. "Until five years ago, I knew the Adirondacks was a place where they made chairs, but that's all I knew about it," Jamie said, as we climbed into his hybrid-electric Toyota Prius. We drove down Lake Shore Road toward the small town of Essex, passing Webb-Royce swamp. "That has long been a birders' mecca; there was a big heron rookery. But then the beavers were trapped out and the water levels plummeted. By protecting the parcel, we're hoping the beavers may recolonize." As he said it, we passed a porcupine dead in the road—a good reminder that wildlife corridors are not an abstraction, that animals are constantly on the move following their own imperatives.

A little farther on, though, we came to something quite different—a beautiful little spread, Black Kettle Farm. "This may be the oldest farm in Essex County," says Jamie. "Now, initially John wanted *everything* to grow back to forest, but there was just too much community spirit here. So it will be a wild farm." The farm property ran from a heavily logged high ridge—which will be left alone to recover its wildness—down to the Boquet River. "Down along the fields we're letting the swales between the meadows go wild. Over on the left is where we grew wheat last year—we sold it all to the mill in town, and to Yannick's bakery in Crown Point. Everything he makes, he makes with Champlain Valley wheat."

And a little farther on, by the nearly nonexistent hamlet of Whallonsburg, we came to another Eddy Foundation property. "Habitat for Humanity asked if they could have land to build a house. And we said, 'Sure, here's a parcel.' But in the lease we disallowed any two-stroke engines, and said they had to leash all their pets so they wouldn't bother the wildlife. And the people have been cool about it. They called us to say they got a Weedwacker—but it was an electric one!"

The Split Rock wildway is still in its infancy, and the Eddy Foundation lacks the money to finish the job. Some of the neighbors seem unmoved by the vision— one of Ivan Boesky's former business partners, for instance, has a big spread and farms it as if he were in Kansas, removing every hedgerow to make life easier for his tractors. But it's an impressive idea, an impressive start, and an impressive example of how people like Davis and Butler can hold true to their ideal—wilderness!—and yet adapt a little to the world around them, and of how they can understand that a small farm can have its own kind of beauty, and a house for someone without much money. "We want a wide swath of real green reaching through the valley," John says. "And around it good selection forestry, good organic farming."

The conversation between the wheatfields of Black Kettle Farm and its expanding hedgerows, between Earth First! and the Eddy Foundation, between the tendency of Vermont and the tendency of the Adirondacks, echoes the conversation between Ed Abbey and the other greatest essayist of the real world in our time, the Kentucky farmer Wendell Berry. Here's my truth: a rootless child of the suburbs, I came to wilderness partly through the written word. Through Abbey, following Bob Marshall and John Muir and Henry Thoreau. And I first came to care about the good *use* of land—forest and field—again less through experience than through books, in particular Berry's. He is, in many ways, the utter opposite of Abbey. One left the Appalachian uplands for the raw West, saying that the "fuzzy hills" of the East made him feel trapped; the other returned from school in California to make his life in the Kentucky farming town where he'd been raised. One, "Cactus Ed," was wildly and rudely funny, irresponsible in marriage, likely to be drunk in the evening or at least to imply that he had been. The other is very nearly solemn in his writing, valuing fidelity above all else. One seemed most alive in motion (his essay on the joys of abusing rental cars is a masterpiece); the other draws his strength from what he has called "sticking." It seemed at first to me as if a reader had to choose one vision or the other. But both appealed enormously to me, and as I got to know both men, they were deeply appealing, too. As it turned out, in fact, they were great fans of each other, attempting on the backs of various books to pin each other with the title of our finest national essayist.

The admiration came, in part, from simple appreciation of craft. "A sort of law at our house is that I should not read an Abbey book after bedtime," Berry once said. "For if I did, I would be apt to laugh loud enough to wake people up." But much more, I think, it stemmed from the sense that they each held part of the puzzle: the iconoclastic, individualistic, rebellious defense of the wild as necessary for our sanity; the communalistic, enduring defense of the pastoral as necessary for our culture. The point is, they were appropriate in different degrees in different places (which, of course, is the great insight of ecology to begin with). Abbey makes intuitive sense in the desert country where he landed, and Berry in his fertile fields.

But both knew they needed at least a smidgen of the other. In his last and greatest novel, *A Fool's Progress,* Abbey's alter ego, dying, makes his way home from the West to the Eastern mountains where he'd grown up, home to his family. His brother finds him as he nears the house, tells him they've been expecting him "for weeks. For years. Come on down to the house now. Supper's almost ready." At which Henry "felt a great bewildered joy rising in his heart; fifty-three years—maybe that was enough after all." For his part, Berry took time from his unceasing defense of the small farm and the small farmer to write, among other things, a passionate and effective defense of Kentucky's Red River Gorge. It was threatened with flooding by a dam in the same way that Abbey's beloved Glen Canyon had been submerged, to generate power and to "provide recreation" for powerboaters. "The Gorge, dammed, would be like *Hamlet* rewritten for the feeble-minded," he said in his book *The Unforeseen Wilderness.* And what do you know—the dam was never built.

At Abbey's funeral, Berry read a poem he'd written for the occasion:

I pass a cairn of stone
Two arm-lengths long and wide
Piled on the steep hillside
By plowmen years ago.
Now oaks and hickories grow
Where the steel coulter passed.
Where human striving ceased
The Sabbath of the trees
Returns and stands and is.

This idea of a reconciliation between the wild and the pastoral is not something I've just worked out. In the last decade or so, conservationists have become more and more aware of the need to work with, not against, traditional users of the land. Partly that's a response to the antienvironmental political mood in Washington, which requires making allies instead of enemies; partly it comes from a growing scientific understanding that, say, good forestry and wolf habitat can overlap. Part of it, too, comes from an increasingly sophisticated sense of the scale of our environmental problems—that protecting wilderness in Vermont is not really an "answer" if it leads directly to the destruction of forests somewhere else for a paper-hungry world. And in some measure it comes, I think, from the sense of pleasure at working at the very human tasks of food and shelter—and community. It's not surprising, anymore, to find some of the nation's most innovative farming and ranching being done on land owned by the Nature Conservancy, whose brief never used to extend past saving endangered species.

But there are very few regions that illustrate the possibilities in as close proximity as this region I am trying to construct across the New York–Vermont border. The two sides of the lake are different—the Adirondacks are higher, with a different geology and hydrology, and a harsher climate. Not a lot harsher, but enough so that most attempts at farming didn't last more than a generation. Vermont is famously pastoral—pick up any calendar. And yet Vermont has some real wildlands. I'd begun my hike in the Breadloaf Wilderness, the state's largest; if a new wilderness bill passes this year, as it should, 2 percent of the state will be designated wilderness, and considerably more is wilderness of the de facto sort. Meanwhile, the Adirondack Park has plenty of honest-to-God residents, who are trying to figure out how they can make their living at the same time and in pretty much the same place as the rest of creation. The line between these places is really more of a blur.

It reminded me of something John Davis had said as we rowed away from the Vermont side, looking back at the broad farmlands of the eastern shore. "There's a lot of little patches of trees there, you know. Just by strategically allowing a few of those fields to grow back to forest, you could link a lot of those shards." You could, that is, Abbeyize a little of the domesticated valley floor, just as preserving Black Kettle farm will Berry a patch of this Split Rock wildway. Blur, not line.

JOHN DAVIS MAY think a little differently than he did at twenty-two. But he doesn't live much differently. His cabin is one room, in a dark hemlock grove above a beaver flow. It's off the grid, as we say these days. But there's no solar power—there's no power at all. Just a woodstove and some oil lamps. No running water, just a privy. No phone line. No driveway, and nothing to put in it. "The Adirondacks are very bike-friendly," he says. If your average American said that, he would mean something like: the Adirondacks are a good place to ride a bike. They have well-paved roads with wide shoulders. What Davis means is, they're a good place to *only* ride a bike. "If you want to live in a wild landscape and not use a car, you couldn't ask for a better place." Meaning that, many times a year, he'll ride twenty miles or so to the base of some high mountain, bushwhack up it, bushwhack back down, and ride home to his cabin. Meaning that when he needs to go to the airport in Burlington so he can fly to California and do some wildlands philanthropy organizing, he rows his bike across the lake, ties up his boat, and pedals forty miles to the terminal. Meaning that he rides the talk.

And meaning that he's in insanely good shape. We push off early in the morning, walking back roads and old fields west, toward Elizabethtown and then the northern edge of the High Peaks. We cross the Boquet River a couple of times, stopping in the morning heat for a swim, and eventually pass underneath the Adirondack Northway, Interstate 87, which thunders overhead. The highway, built in the 1960s, runs from Albany past Plattsburgh to the Canadian border. It slices through the eastern Adirondacks, just on the edge of the High Peaks, and Davis calls it "the worst ecological disaster in Adirondack history," worse even than the massive clearcutting at the end of the nineteenth century. Partly that's because it opened up the territory for tens of thousands of new second-home owners: what had been a ten-hour trip from the city was now five or six hours. But the Northway also serves as a physical barrier for any animal trying to move east to west across this region. Lake Champlain freezes more winters than not, making migration relatively simple. But the trucks keep coming down 87 all night. "When they built it, they put in some token wildlife tunnels," says Davis. "But what's using them is mostly people on ATVs." A key portion of the Split Rock wildway he's trying to build will be the corridor where the north branch of the Boquet passes beneath the highway—if a bear or a moose or a wolf makes it through there, she's managed to pass one of the worst obstacles between the Atlantic in Maine and the shore of Lake

Ontario. But at the moment the fence that should exclude motor vehicles is down, and signs of dirt bikes are everywhere.

This day is the hottest yet of this trip, and it ends with a couple of uphill miles along Route 9, heat kicking off the blacktop, pickups dopplering by. Which makes it all the sweeter when we finally reach the trailhead, and within a few short steps drop into another world— the transition is as abrupt as if we'd gone from a hot Manhattan sidewalk through a door into a hushed and air-conditioned movie theater. It's a real, deep Adirondack woods, this back side of Giant Mountain. After several hours of pavement, the thick red carpet of hemlock needles feels like a trampoline beneath my boots. We walk perhaps a mile and then make camp along a little stream, with a pool just big enough to submerge in.

From his small pack John hauls a plastic bag of granola—it emerges that this is pretty much all he eats while in the woods. "A stove might break, and I'm not very good at fixing things," he says, which is almost certainly not true. It's more likely that a stove is . . . not strictly necessary, kind of like a car or electricity or a phone. I've been dragging my stove every step of the way along this journey, and though it's called a Whisperlite, in fact it's a pretty hefty chunk of steel, especially once you factor in the bottle full of white gas, which if you start thinking about it probably connects me straight back to the Persian Gulf. I'm grateful for my soup and my hot chocolate, but the pack felt awfully heavy the last few miles. I fell asleep considering whether, all in all, I'd allowed myself to get a little top-heavy with possessions— with needs—over the last couple of decades. Considering what it would be like to live in a cabin in the hemlocks with a privy out back. Or at least what it would be like to be carrying twenty pounds on my back instead of fifty. At the trailhead where we'd left the road, there'd been a sign announcing that Giant Mountain, which we planned to reach by noon the next day, was 3,327 vertical feet above us, which is quite a ways to tote your perhaps not fully considered way of life. I slept a bit fitfully, even before a crashing thunderstorm hit around midnight.

THE FIRST FEW miles in the morning are often the sweetest part of a day's hike, and so it was this day. The thunderstorm had, temporarily, washed a little of the humidity out of the air, and the trail climbed gently upward through a lovely forest, with some big stands of old, shaggy yellow birch. We were alone in this woods, at least as far as other humans. Though the High Peaks see a lot of hikers, almost all of them come in from Route 73, the main road that bisects the mountains. That means almost everyone climbed Giant from the southern side, where we'd be descending this afternoon. By contrast, this trail was hiked just enough that it was easy to follow, but it hadn't turned into a muddy trench the way some of the busier paths do. As we hiked, John and I chatted about old friends—Walkin' Jim Stoltz, who bushwhacked every year from Mexico to Canada through the most deserted territory, following goat paths and writing songs on the guitar strapped to his pack. Or the Maine writer Gary Lawless, who was poetry editor for the *Earth First! Journal* and who titled one of his collections *Caribouddist.* So the walking was easy, and by ten we'd reached the morning's first objective, a knob called Owl's Head.

Owl's Head stuck up in the middle of this wilderness area like an . . . owl's head. We rested atop a boulder and took in the 360-degree view, which was composed entirely of mountains, rocky slides, climbing ridges, and trees, with the single exception of a fire tower visible on Hurricane Mountain to our north. Quoting George Wuerthner, another old friend and outdoors writer, John said, "It's hard to match the wildness of the viewscape from an Adirondack mountaintop. Out West you can almost always see a clearcut." (Which is true. I can remember climbing Washington state's great volcano, Mount Rainier. We set out for the summit under a full moon just after midnight, and the view was sublime, endless peaks in every direction. But as the sun came up, I could suddenly see with sad precision the exact boundaries of the national park—that was where the checkerboard of clearcuts stopped.) It always rouses us Adirondack chauvinists to hear any comparison like this. We want it recognized that we're in country just as tough and rugged as those North Dakota badlands or those Montana High Plains or those Idaho river canyons. We're out West, too, except back East.

But the very idea of being out by yourself in capital-W Wilderness raises a whole other set of philosophical questions. Ed Abbey and Wendell Berry, as I have said, had a pleasant set of discussions over the years about the relative use of leaving land alone and managing it well, and concluded, sensibly, that some of each, in its proper place, was just what was called for. (The sensibleness of their conclusion is in no way undermined by the fact that the larger Economy continues at breakneck pace to wreck both wild places and small-scale farms in the name of More and Cheaper.) But a few years later, in the 1990s, the ground of debate, and its temper, shifted. The question now became: Is there any such thing as wilderness? And is trying to protect it a pointless delusion?

I hesitate slightly to wade right back into a more intellectual dispute on what I intended to be a pleasant walk in the woods. But when you walk through wilderness, you walk through an idea, and in fact you walk through an idea that has its roots partly in the Adirondacks. Five or six days hence, if all goes well, I will bushwhack through the wilderness within a mile or two of the cabin where a man named Howard Zahniser spent his summers, enjoying the Adirondack scenery and drafting the federal wilderness statute, the one that stated: "A wilderness, in contrast with those areas where man and his works dominate the landscape, is hereby recognized as an area where the earth and its community of life are untrammeled by man, where man himself is a visitor who does not remain." Passed by Congress in 1964, that language may represent the single most philosophical stand our legislators have ever taken; it has also allowed the protection of tens of millions of acres free from (except where political concessions were made) cattle grazing, mining, tree-cutting, roadbuilding, dirt-bike riding, and pretty much every other intrusion except wandering around on your own two feet. For most of the next three decades, the battle over wilderness was pretty much between those people who wanted more of it and those who wanted to graze, mine, cut, build, and roar around.

In the mid-1990s, a new critique began to emerge. Its most prominent advocate was an environmental historian named William Cronon, who had already written several truly classic books—most notably *Changes in the Land,* the story of how both the Indians and the settlers had thoroughly and permanently reshaped the landscape of New England. Instead of imagining that Native Americans had inhabited a primeval Eastern paradise that colonists corrupted, he said, his project was "to locate a nature which is within rather than without history." So it was not completely novel for him to argue, in a paper he published in 1995 called "The Trouble with Wilderness," that land truly "untrammeled by man" was unlikely to be found, and that the insistence on a kind of wilderness purity was in fact doing the environmental movement harm by leading to a neglect of more-ordinary (and much larger) landscapes. That, in fact, by going out of their way to excise humans from these sacred cathedrals, environmentalists were alienating people from the land. Worshiping wilderness, said Cronon, "we reproduce the dualism that sets humanity and nature at opposite poles. We thereby leave ourselves little hope of discovering what an ethical, sustainable, honorably human place in nature might actually look like."

Now, talk like this excited a number of academics, because it fit reasonably well with the deconstructionist agenda of the time. A generation of thinkers had become used to the idea of looking at a book and saying it was, in and of itself, nothing more than a reflection of its author's subjectivities, something to be "read" with an eye not to plot or character or language but to gender, class, and other such categories. A few years earlier, a feminist academic named Donna Haraway had scored a great coup with an article that argued that humans themselves were, happily, on the verge of finally becoming totally unnatural: cyborgs, connected to computers and soon to be genetically engineered, and thus liberated from the idea that we were "men" or "women" or even "human beings" and hence from the idea that we had to act in certain ways. To them, Cronon seemed to be saying that wilderness, too, was not exactly real, that it was mere construction, simply another category. That I was hiking not through the Giant Mountain Wilderness, but through an abstraction—and perhaps even a dangerous abstraction, one that kept me from dealing with much more serious environmental problems.

Wilderness defenders, predictably, reacted badly to this news. Partly they thought: Damn, this is all we need. Having soldiered on through Ronald Reagan and James Watt, through the attacks (literal attacks, often) of the Western antienvironmental "sagebrush rebellion," and the billions of dollars thrown against them by timber and mining interests, now we have to contend with a bunch of professors (who had held their key conference in Irvine, California, a place about as spiritually far removed from the wild as it is possible to get) telling us not to bother? Cronon was seen to be giving aid and comfort to the enemy, but in a particularly sneaky way. He'd quoted the poet Gary Snyder (along with Abbey and Berry the third star by which I navigated) as saying "A person with a clear heart and open mind can experience the wilderness anywhere on earth. It is a quality of one's own consciousness." But Snyder—in a special issue of *Wild Earth,* edited by John Davis—said he'd been quoted out of context. "I must confess I'm getting a bit grumpy about the dumb arguments being put forth by high-paid intellectual types in which they are trying to knock Nature, knock the people who value nature, and still come out smart and progressive," he wrote. In general, then, environmentalist sentiment was: Give us a break. Call it what you will, we're out here protecting landscapes big enough for animals to flourish and for people to occasionally get a little lost in, and that's a good thing, not a bad one.

To his credit, I think Cronon recognized that truth largely from the start. "It is not the things we label as wilderness that are the problem—for nonhuman nature and large tracts of the natural world do deserve protection—but rather what we ourselves mean when we used that label," he wrote. And he's gone on to write wonderful and sensitive investigations of both the human and the natural meaning of particular places. In general, the controversy died away. We could still stand here on Owl's Head in midsummer 2003 and say, "This is a wild place."

But I don't think the questions about wilderness and its meaning will in fact stay tamped down for long. A few years before Cronon, I wrote a book called *The End of Nature* that grew in part from my years in the Adirondacks and that raised a somewhat similar challenge to the idea of the wild. It was the first book for a general audience about global warming, and half of it was pretty much straight science reporting: here's how much the temperature is going to go up, here's how we might rein it in a little. But the other half explored the reasons that the prospect of massive climate change made me so sad—basically because it threatened my newfound love affair with the wild world. I had found the place I belonged, I knew that in my bones. But suddenly the meaning of that place was in question. Say people, in their carelessness, pushed the temperature up four or five degrees this century, which is the current middle-of-the-road prediction. In that case, Owl's Head might never overlook another real winter, just one long mud season. In the fall, instead of the birch and beech turning yellow and orange in this vast wood, those trees would be dead, replaced if at all by the drab brown of oak and hickory. In the first warm days of March, there'd be no maples left to bleed their sweet sap. Since it's already started getting warmer, is this still the Adirondacks, still the Champlain Valley? Was our place wild, or natural, anymore? For that matter, was *any* place? The peculiar physics of global warming mean, in fact, that the North and South Poles will be hardest hit—that is, the places that really are free of any other human history, really wild if any place is wild, might just as well be in the middle of the eastern megalopolis or the SoCal suburbs.

I got in less trouble from wilderness advocates than Cronon did,[2] in part because I was clearly one of them, and in part because I was catching so much hell from oil

2. I did not escape their wrath entirely, however. Google allows one instantly to dredge up sentiments like the following, a quote from Mike Medbury of the Idaho Conservation League in a November 1996 issue of *High Country News:* "This whole Bill McKibben Bill Cronon thing about the death of nature and the death of wilderness as a concept is utter horseshit. These guys are getting into this heady philosophy about wilderness; they're trying to deconstruct us or something. I would just like to put them out there in it somewhere and see what they say."

companies for suggesting that we needed to overhaul industrial civilization. But the argument persists. It's not easy to see what the idea of something apart from man, something untrammeled, will amount to in a globally warmed, genetically engineered world, a world totally reshaped by our recklessness and our shortsighted desire. Mightn't we just give up on the whole thing and go play video games?

For me, though, the idea that there's no such thing as pure wilderness has made the *relative wild* all the more precious. Yes, Cronon's right, and so was I—there's no place that isn't touched by man. I have a friend, Curt Stager, who teaches biology at Paul Smith's College, the only four-year school in the Adirondacks. Curt spent years out with his students looking for a pristine Adirondack Lake, one that hadn't been sterilized by acid rain, one whose sediment cores didn't show telltale signs of logging or roadbuilding in the watershed. He never found one, and he had three thousand to choose from. And now it rains or snows or doesn't on those lakes in some small measure because of the kind of cars we drive or the ways we heat our homes. In 2003, scientists summed up a review of many different studies—studies of leaf-out in the spring, of migration dates, of hibernation patterns— and concluded that because of global warming, spring was coming seven days earlier at this latitude than just a few decades before.

But it's precisely *because* of such things that we badly need more wild, not less. For pragmatic reasons: if plants and animals are going to need to move north against the rising temperature, we have to give them as much room, and as many corridors, as we can carve out (assuming, that is, that you buy the basic conservationist argument that plants and animals are worth preserving). But beyond that, we need more wild for *human* reasons: we need to set aside land from our use simply to prove to ourselves that we can do it, that we don't need to be in control of everything around us. The battle for the future is precisely between those who are willing to engineer every organism for our convenience, who will countenance the radical change of our climate rather than risk any damage to our cosseted and swaddled Economy, and those who are willing to say there is something other than us that counts. Wilderness and Gandhian nonviolence were the two most potentially revolutionary ideas of the twentieth century, precisely because they were the two most humble: they imagine a whole different possibility for people.

There's another, less stern, reason we need the wild, too, of course, and that's for sheer comfort. I'd hiked Giant several times in my life—the best was on the first anniversary of meeting my wife, Sue, when we walked up in a gray fog with a bottle of champagne, only to have the clouds instantly part as we sat on the summit, pulled away like stage curtains to reveal the late-September glory below. Probably because of that good memory, I headed back on one of the darker days of my life, the morning after the elections of 1994, when Newt Gingrich swept into control of the House on the strength of his Contract with America. It seemed to me as if the nation I loved had finally gone totally crazy, that it had settled for the most gimcrack and transparent kind of fraud, and that a kind of intolerance was settling over the land that would eventually make life scary for people like myself, who seemed suddenly not critics of the ruling order, but *dissidents.* Anyway, a hard day's solitary hike was enough to restore a bit of equilibrium, and Gingrich landed harder than I did in the end—but a world without Giant Mountain, or a Giant Mountain with a toll road on it, or a gondola, or an ATV mosh pit, seems more worth fighting against than ever. "Forever wild," as the New York constitution puts it, even if "wild" means a little less than it used to, and if "forever" seems somewhat shorter.

THE GOOD THING about philosophical speculation is that it can carry you right up a mountain, even a steep-sided, mossy-rocked one like this. We spilled out on the summit before I'd expected it, and now for the first time could see way south and west across the expanse of the High Peaks and the spread of the lower Adirondacks far beyond. Mount Marcy and the Algonquin ridge and the

Great Range beckoned across the valley of the Au Sable River; looking east, it was easy to trace the route I'd come right from the Breadloaf ridge of the Green Mountains. And I could see the rest of my track laid out before me, too—Hunters Pass beneath the Dixes, and the Hoffman Notch wilderness beyond, and past that the deep and remote Adirondack forests of the Hudson headwaters. I pulled last night's storm-drenched tent from the pack and laid it across the rocks to dry, and ate my lunch, and congratulated myself on reaching the literal high point of the journey, 4,627 feet. It's all downhill from here, I thought, which as it turned out was one of those brags you're better off not making.

WE SET OFF on our descent, against a steady stream of hikers climbing up on the more usual route. Many were would-be 46ers, checking off another of the peaks on the list first compiled by Bob Marshall when he was a young man spending his summers in Saranac Lake. A staunch hiker, he and his friends tried to climb every high mountain in the park. Forty-six, he said, topped 4,000 feet, and these became the grail. (Better measurements showed he included four that didn't belong, and missed one that did—but myth proved more rugged than mere measurement, and his list still holds.) Many of the peaks on the list, Giant included, are glorious; others are grim marches to flat-topped mountains with no views that would never be climbed, were they not on the official itinerary. It's simple to make a little sport of the 46ers, especially since some people, upon finishing the list the first time, set in trying to climb them all in the winter, or to stand on every peak at midnight, or to visit each in the rain. But the quest serves two purposes: by providing that American necessity, a goal, it gives people a good excuse to get out into wild country; and it makes sure that the other thousand or so mountains are almost totally ignored simply because they're too low. If you know an Adirondack summit is 3,950 feet high, then you know you'll have it all to yourself.

In fact, as is often the case, describing something turns it into a magnet. Marshall was a born salesman—on top of one Adirondack peak he came up with the idea for The Wilderness Society, which in turn led the drive for the 1964 federal statute, relying all the time on the inherent appeal of the word. The 3 million acres of "forever wild" land in the Adirondacks are divided into two main designations, "wild forest" and "wilderness." The differences are very minor, having to do with grandfathered jeep trails and the like—but because wilderness sounds sexier, those areas almost invariably draw more hikers. Some conservationists worry that the High Peaks Wilderness in particular gets too much use, and there are periodic attempts to limit the number of hikers going up mountains like this one—require permits, some say, or build more parking lots and facilities elsewhere in the park to disperse use. But in fact one of the glories of the Adirondacks is that the high granite vacuums up most of the visitors, leaving the rest of the park to the creatures.

There were more than enough visitors wandering up Giant today, including at least one group communicating very loudly over walkie-talkies with other members of their party who were roughly, oh, forty feet away. I fear I must have been thinking of some cutting remark to make to John, because bad karma grabbed me by the ankle and sent me down hard on a steep rock shelf. Actually, the first part of the fall wasn't so bad—but a half-second later the full weight of my pack slammed into my back, sending me eight or ten feet farther down the slope and leaving me with blood streaming from both knees. No permanent damage, but I was sore and hot and grumpy as we plodded down the trail. I was, I think, feeling my age, which is the only bitter thing about hiking peaks you've hiked many times before. The trail never seemed this long before, and it didn't help that granola-fed John was leaping lightly from rock to rock.

Thank heaven the path spills out on Route 73 right across from Chapel Pond, which is among the loveliest places in the park. In the nineteenth century, apparently, ranks of artists would stand by its shores almost every day, lined up behind their easels, trying to capture the rocky slides and steep, birchy draws above the pond itself. In our time this spot speaks most loudly to rock climbers—whatever the season, there's always a van or two alongside the road, and a few specks moving up the pitches. In winter, when a dozen waterfalls ice up, the crowds of climbers really gather. But today I wasn't paying much attention. All I wanted was to take off my pack and go for a nice long swim in the pond, kicking just fast enough that the blood trailing off my knees wouldn't attract too many leeches.

John had to be somewhere the next morning, so he actually allowed a friend to come pick him up in an automobile. I reminded him how such a contraption worked—the seat belt, the window crank—and then, feeling virtuous, gimped off to the east on the two-lane for half a mile till I came to the next trailhead. This one led south, and in less than a mile passed Round Pond, where I made camp for the night.

Round Pond is a lovely sheet of water set in a perfect forest bowl, and tonight it was graced by three loons, not to mention a small band of Christian college students. Nice as it is, however, it must be said that its name leaves a bit to be desired. I mean, come on, Round Pond. I've swum in at least four Round Ponds in the Adirondacks, and I bet there are fifty more. Not to mention dozens of Mud Ponds, and Loon Lakes in every direction. As a rule, Adirondack place names lack distinction. The problem, I think, is that there simply weren't enough people to create enough history; even the Indians mostly used the central Adirondacks as a hunting ground, preferring to site their villages in the warmer, more fertile land around Lake Champlain to the east, Lake Ontario to the West, the St. Lawrence to the north, and the Mohawk River to the south. They gave good names to some things—Tahawus, or Cloud Splitter, may have been their title for the Adirondacks' loftiest peak (or it may have been dreamed up in the nineteenth century by some romantic writer). But the first white guys who climbed it didn't bother with romance at all, naming it for the undistinguished governor William Marcy who had paid for their trip (and coined the phrase "spoils system").

At least Marcy was a *name,* though—for the most part, this is anonymous land, much of it named as if it had been inventoried by a warehouse clerk. There's First Lake, Second Lake, on up at least through Fourteenth Lake. There are so many Blue Mountains and Clear Ponds that the map index reads like a Beijing phone directory. As a result, I take it upon myself to occasionally rechristen particular spots with names I can remember. Tonight, tuneless hymns were drifting across from the campers on the far shore of Round Pond, an off-key bleating shamed by the pure clear laughter of the loons. "Shall We Gather at the River" is one of my favorites, but not in a Gregorian chant. From now on, I'll call it Bird-Beats-Baptist Pond.

✸

THE NEXT DAY'S destination was Elk Lake, and I'd been looking forward to the hike. But that's because I'd mis-read the map. From the top of Giant, I could see straight through Hunter's Pass, which crossed the height of land on this day's journey. It was a low pass—3,200 feet on the map, which meant that my high point for the day would be almost 2,000 feet lower than the summit of Giant. And I knew much of the trail—I'd gone winter camping along the Boquet one Christmas week.

A longer look at the map, however, would have reminded me that the trail didn't actually go through Hunter's Pass. Because of an intervening piece of private property, hikers are forced to climb almost to the summit of Dix Mountain, fifteen hundred feet above the pass. And what a climb—this little-used trail was essentially hand over hand, a shinny up roots and cracks. Kind of fun, I'm sure, on a cool fall day with your lunch in your pocket, but kind of not fun on a hot and humid morning with too much crammed in a backpack. I went through most of my water on the ascent; then the climb down was very nearly as tough, especially since I was still gin-gerly from yesterday's fall. And then the long walk out. I should have stopped at one of the creeks and pumped myself some more water with the filter I'd carefully car-ried all this way, but I'd dropped into a kind of walking stupor. I'll just keep going till Elk Lake, I'd tell myself—

there's water there. Hell, there's a big lodge there. They probably have *ice* water. Maybe ice *cream*.

And indeed by two-thirty in the afternoon the trail spit me out onto the access road to the Elk Lake Lodge, one of the Adirondacks' finest hostelries. What I'd forgotten, however, was just how fine. There were signs *everywhere* reminding hikers that they should stick to the trails, that the lodge was For Guests Only, that they shouldn't pass this point without permission, on and on and on. I have no doubt—well, not too much doubt—that they would have received me civilly if I had walked the half-mile to their porch. But I was suddenly conscious of just how smelly, muddy, blood-flecked, and dusty I actually was. So I headed the other way, walking the four-mile road out to the Blue Ridge Highway. That dirt road, essentially the driveway to the Elk Lake Lodge, passes a couple of lakes, but these too are plastered with No Trespassing signs. In fact, in under two miles I counted 155 posted signs along the road—Guests Only, No Stopping. There was not a spot along the road out of sight of such a sign, and it worked—I just kept trudging, parched and a little sullen, thinking the kinds of thoughts that English peasants must have thought when nobles fenced off all the good hunting grounds.

On the other hand, it reminded me to be truly thankful for the 3 million acres of public land in the park, a landmass half the size of Vermont open to absolutely everyone, no questions asked. By tonight I'd be back on that land, and I could stay on it pretty much all the way home.

Anyway, my weariness set me up for one of those moments that you wouldn't fully appreciate under any other circumstance. Reaching the highway (if that's what you want to call the Blue Ridge Road—it is two lanes, but it's about as busy as the post office on Sunday), I turned left because in the distance I could see a low building with a sign out front. Real estate? Chain-saw-carved bears? Or, just maybe, food and drink? It took me twenty minutes to get there, but when I did—well, it was like some kind of desert mirage that turns out to be real. Odd but real. The establishment was called the Adirondack Bison Company, and indeed there was a herd of bison out back, in a small meadow carved out of the woods that stretched for miles in every direction. That was queer enough, but there was also a deck overlooking the bison pasture, and on it was one of those telescopes like you'd see at Niagara Falls, where if you put in a quarter you could watch the bison standing in the dust very close up. You could make out every bison hair! But I didn't do any bison-gazing for about half an hour. Instead, I went into the tiny store, which featured four things: vast quantities of bison jerky, a cooler full of Snapple, some garden produce, and a table piled with homemade desserts on Styrofoam plates wrapped in Saran Wrap. Without saying a word I drained three lemonades and ate two slabs of chocolate cake and a piece of blueberry pie (fifty cents apiece)—it was as if every food dream of the last few days had somehow managed to assemble itself here on this lonely road, with a herd of bison thrown in for good measure.

My belly comfortably distended, I sat on the porch and chatted with the proprietors, who manifestly had not been born in California. They were not New Age bison-herders. They were people who had lived here all their lives and thought there might be some money in bison. Or maybe they just liked bison—abstract questions didn't get very far. So we chatted about the news of the central Adirondacks ("A bear climbed a power pole over to Long Lake last night. Electrocuted himself. Knocked out power to the entire town.") and discussed the peculiar buying habits of tourists ("city folks like big kernels on their corn").

So, I said, is there a restaurant around here somewhere where I can get a bison steak?

The rancher looked at me a little funny, as if the thought hadn't occurred to him. And then he said, "Well, they have it over to Vermont." Which struck me as the punch line for a long, complicated joke I'd been telling for the last ten days.

I CAMPED THAT NIGHT on the northern edge of the Hoffman Notch Wilderness, along a stream known locally as "the Branch." It began to rain around midnight, and it was still coming down with some vigor the next morning, when Chris Shaw joined me for the day's trek.

The Hoffman Notch wilderness is quintessential Adirondacks, much more typical than the High Peaks country I'd been traveling the last few days. It's pretty big—36,000 acres—and it's very lonely. Because the peaks stay under 4,000 feet, the trail register shows just fifty or sixty people a summer hiking the one trail that bisects the area. Except during hunting season, I imagine that the number who wander very far off that single trail might be counted in the single digits. It's empty, trackless country, unless you count the tracks of other creatures. Predictably, the main point of interest along the one trail carries the compelling name of Big Marsh; the biggest lake in the wilderness is known as Big Pond.

And Chris Shaw was the perfect person to hike it with, for there's probably no one who's traveled more widely and lived more deeply in these mountains. He came to the Adirondacks as a young man, and over the next decades worked as a camp caretaker, raft guide, ski-lift operator—always in a different town, a different corner.[3] All the time he was writing stories and novels and articles, and eventually he ended up as editor of *Adirondack Life,* turning what had been a low-wattage tourist rag into an award-winning regional magazine. One of the ways he did that was to

3. One thing he didn't do was record a lot of albums of Adirondack folk songs—that's another Christopher Shaw.

encourage actual reporting, which of course got him fired eventually, when he offended one (subsequently indicted) local power broker—but no matter, since he's gone on to write fine books since, and explore ever more deeply into these mountains.

So we walked up the Hoffman Notch Brook, admiring many small cataracts and moss-slicked boulders. When the trail leveled out at Big Marsh, the overgrowth was so thick across the trail that we might as well have been bushwhacking. The rain had ceased, but we hardly noticed, for every step brushed us against boughs freighted with water. Our rain pants and Gore-Tex jackets were soon soaked through—their main effect was merely to trap our sweat on this humid afternoon. I've been wetter in my life, but I've never been damper.

Never mind, though, because Chris talked as we walked. He's lived, as I said, across the park, from Stony Creek in the southeast to Rainbow Lake in the north, which are somewhat farther apart than Boston and Hartford. But, he insisted, there was something consistently Adirondack about them all. "The quality of the light is essentially the same. And the general feeling of place. It's continuous throughout the Blue Line—it's amazing how continuous it is. When you start to get up on the massif, the air changes and the light changes. Sometimes I wonder where it comes from—the rock, maybe, or the combination of the rock and the altitude and the vegetation. There's a very special time in the late summer, late

August say, toward dusk. You're along shore on a lake or river, along that distinctive shoreline of mixed heath and rock. And all of the features click, fall in place for me. When that happens all at once it's like seeing your own name by accident in print, or catching sight of your handwriting on a piece of paper where you didn't expect to see it. There's a very powerful feeling of identity."

But something else unified Shaw's sense of the Adirondacks, especially when he first arrived around 1970: "The memories of the old timers, those who were still around. The people who had really lived the industrial life of the Adirondacks, who had made livings off the resources of this place, back when you could still do that. The people who had worked in the woods or in the garnet mines or the tanneries. Who had farmed and failed, or farmed and moved on to other things. I think there must have been about fifteen of us who arrived more or less simultaneously from the outside in Stony Creek in the 1970s. As often happened in those back-to-the-land days, there was a standoff for a while with the locals that pretty quickly changed to accommodation and then to affection. It was as if a lot of those men and women had almost been waiting their whole lives for the audience we represented. We sat spellbound for four or five years, and we heard about the old days. Learned the logging songs not from some folk CD, but from people who'd sung them in the logging camps. It meant a whole lot to us, coming from the suburbs. All my life I wondered where real life was, and so to be welcomed into their circle was a great honor. There was a kind of authenticity in the life they led. Less in our life, but it grew to have some."

Five or six years after the newcomers arrived, those old-timers started to die. "It came as a great shock to me," Shaw says. "I remember one guy, George Ardnt. He'd been in both world wars—in World War I he was in the cavalry, down on the Mexican border, chasing Pancho Villa with General Pershing. In World War II he'd been an Army cook in Europe. Mostly he was a horsetrader, a guide, a caretaker, a trapper, a hunter. One day in 1976, I remember driving home from a canoe trip. I came past the town beach in Long Lake and saw his truck there. I knew what he and his friend Mo West were doing—it was a hot day, they were asleep in their undershirts, there was a bottle of whiskey no doubt. And I knew what they were going to do when it cooled off a little—they liked to go bullheading out there in the lake, some little bay they liked. I mean, I knew the pattern of their lives pretty well. And then I found out the next day that he'd died out there in the boat. After that it was like a domino effect—after that it was Mo West, Grant Richards, Jackie Perkins. Some real beauties, people I miss. It wasn't so much just themselves, but there was a quality of memory that I believe informed the place. It was tangible. It was in the air, it made the place what it was for me. When those memories were extinguished— well, I remember the guys, but I don't remember what they remember. Their children have sort of become part of the general American television culture. They're not as place-defined as the old timers. The loss of them and their memories has changed the place. It's as if someone came and knocked down a thousand-acre stand of mature timber, as far as I'm concerned. It reminds me of this great story by Borges, who writes about the last real Saxon in England dying in a stable in England, the last guy who remembers the rites of Wodin in the Christian era. With the death of that last pagan Saxon, a whole world of memory is lost. That's what I felt like when some of those old men and women started to drop off."

By now we'd gotten past Big Marsh, and the trail had opened up some—it was an old logging road by the looks of it, from the time fifty or a hundred years before when the big hemlocks and pines had first been cut. People still work at some of the old occupations—cutting trees on the half of the park still in private hands is probably the most common job—and they've pioneered a few new occupations. (Shaw himself helped pioneer the park's white-water rafting industry.) But in general I think he's right. The days of the battle to carve a living from these woods are in some ways past. People here often live on money from away, either in the form of government payments or on their own money accumulated before they got here, or on the money that tourists and second-home buyers bring with them. Making a living off the land is no longer the common denominator of Adirondack life, and one result is that much of the land, or at least those parts of it below 4,000 feet, get less use with each passing year. The number of hunters drops annually, since many boys would rather do their shooting in computer games. And all of that is a sadness, precisely because, as Shaw says, there was an authenticity to those human lives that no longer can be matched.

In compensation, however, something else is slowly happening: the woods are growing in to a kind of deep and anonymous majesty. The nonhuman thrives. Here in the Hoffman Notch, logging once ruled. And when it did, other things suffered. The beaver had been extirpated from the Adirondack park by the beginning of the twentieth century, when state wildlife officials reintroduced a few pairs they'd trapped in Canada. Here, as in every other little watershed in the park, the beavers have by now completely reclaimed their territory—there's not a stream I know of that could support a lodge that doesn't have one. Behind their dams, new wetlands back up every year, their muck the single richest biome around. They buzz with dragonflies; frogs turn them earsplitting in the spring. And it's not just small animals: even the big ones, most of them, have returned. The moose have slowly wandered back in during the last fifteen or twenty years, and as we made our moist way through Hoffman Notch, we kept an eye peeled. It was a moosy spot, and if we didn't see one this day, we could have. Which in a tangible way makes this place richer, too.

For me, the ecological story of the Adirondacks is more interesting precisely because it's *not* virgin wilderness. At one point or another, most of it has been cut over, sometimes pretty heavily. And yet, on purpose and by accident, this is one area where people have taken a step back. And nature has responded to that gesture. This is second-chance wilderness—not Eden, but something better. It's the Alaska, the Ngorongoro crater, the Galápagos not of creation but of *redemption*. No place on the planet has restored itself so thoroughly in the last century; while much of the rest of the Earth was turning from green to brown, it was going the other way. And so it produces an emotion at least as important as the sweet nostalgia that comes with remnant virgin wilderness. It signals to the rest of a deeply scarred world that, where we can figure out ways to back off a little, nature still retains some power of renewal. As we wandered farther south along the trail, the trees kept getting bigger, the understory more open, the beech trees more bear-clawed. Barbara McMartin, the obsessive chronicler of all things Adirondack, says in one of her guidebooks that this is among "the most stately mixed forests in the Adirondacks, making you wonder if it has ever been logged." A century hence, if we are lucky, people won't even wonder anymore. They'll just assume it's always been that way. They'll be wrong, of course, and in their error they'll miss much of the human history that Shaw remembers. But as errors go, it will be a sweet one nonetheless.

TO GET AN IDEA of what a century can do to a tree, all you need is to walk to the trail's southern end, in what was once the small settlement of Loch Muller. A truly giant white pine shades the turnaround, and from it hangs this hand-lettered sign:

On this site in year 1845 this pine tree, a sapling of twelve years, was transplanted by me, at the age of twelve years. Seventy-five years I have watched and protected it. In my advancing years it has given me rest and comfort. Woodman spare that tree, touch not a single bough. In youth it sheltered me, and I'll protect it now.

PASCAL P. WARREN, JUNE 14, 1920

NOT ALL THAT much has changed around Loch Muller since Mr. Warren left his plea. A massive new vacation home hangs over the small lake, but the rest of the road is pretty much as it's been for a long time: poor, a few trailers, scattered hunting camps. We're beginning to come into my country, down out of the High Peaks and into the central Adirondacks.

Unlike most North American mountain ranges, where settlement is heaviest south of the big peaks, the central Adirondacks are big and lonely, sparsely settled on the fringes, largely given over to big, unbroken blocks of state land and timber company property. Loch Muller shades into Irishtown and Pottersville and Olmstedville, and a little to the west into Newcomb and Minerva— none of them particularly prosperous or well-known, all of them worried about how much longer they'll be able to hold on to their schools, their stores. The glamorous mountains and lakes are a world away: Saranac Lake or Lake Placid with their CEOs arriving by private jet for a few weeks at "camp" in the summer. My mother's family grew up in West Virginia, and to me this landscape has always seemed closer to Appalachia than to New England. Closer geographically, with its many ridges and hollows; closer culturally, with an ingrained underclass of poverty; closer politically, with none of the strong tradition of town meeting, of civic involvement.

And yet, if there is a more beautiful land, I don't know it. Once I was writing the text for a book of aerial photographs, and the photographer, Alex MacLean, took me up in his tiny plane for a look at my own backyard. What struck me (apart from the terror of riding in a plane with a pilot who spent the whole time leaning all the way out his window with a camera) was the sheer unbroken scale of the forest. The little town roads wound along the edges, but mostly it was unrelieved green.

Too, despite its small population, it contains some of the most remarkable people I've ever met. The people of this territory are backward—which is to say they're only a generation or two removed from knowing how to take care of themselves. Self-sufficiency remains a living memory, although, as Shaw suggests, that memory dims. Still, since almost no one can make a living doing just one thing, the average Adirondacker has many more talents than the average American. Today, for instance, Nick Avignon joined me for a walk through the woods to a place called (I warned you) Stony Pond. Nick, in my experience, can make absolutely anything. When one of his clients wants a stone wall for her summer home, he builds it, by hand and as beautifully as you could ever want. His shop at home is full of tables and desks he's finished—mortise-and-tenon joints, no nails in sight. For a while he worked with Pete Hornbeck, the great canoe-builder of this region, who has taught himself to make Kevlar knockoffs of nineteenth-century Adirondack canoe designs. (My solo boat weighs about fifteen pounds, and it attaches with a couple of wingnuts to my backpack frame, and it's my pride and joy.) In the winter Nick teaches cross-country skiing at one of the local resorts (he used to be a national-caliber downhill racer), and in the spring he plants a massive garden for another affluent family so it will be in full abundance when they arrive for the summer. He does it all quietly and easily and gracefully.

We walk quietly today, talking about family (his wife, Jackie, was our Lamaze teacher) and about old hikes we've taken in the past and grand hikes we're planning for the future. It's a quiet day, nothing spectacular except the mushrooms sprouting obscenely in this wet summer, but quietly *grand,* just like this country. This would be a good place for an interlude of real nature writing, but I am, as you have doubtless already gathered, an incompetent naturalist. Beyond the obvious—trillium, loon, monarch—names tend to slip from my memory. I love walking with good naturalists in the woods, eagerly taking in their descriptions. But each such outing is as exciting as the one before, because I've managed to forget most of what I learned. I'm sure I've been introduced to the yellow-throated whatever on a dozen occasions, but each time it's as if we'd never met. It's *impressions* that linger with me, the sense of the woods as a whole—the relief, the density, the changing feel underfoot and overhead. If you dropped me from a helicopter here and asked me the date, I could give you a pretty good guess—not from the wildflowers out on the forest floor, but from the color of the leaves. The vibrating, nearly neon green of spring has dropped away; we're now approaching the leathery deep green of high summer, which will steadily deepen further until—three weeks or so from now—the first maples along the swampy edges will, overnight, start to show a band of red along the leaf edge. It's the *general,* the *trend,* the *feeling* that somehow sticks with me.

❊

THE WALKING'S GETTING easier day by day. Partly that's
because I'm through with the big mountains and the
high passes. The trails now mostly follow creeks and
streams. And partly it's because every hour brings me
more into my home country. There's always a certain
stress that goes with the adventure of backpacking in less
familiar terrain: how far to the campsite? Where's the
water? On home ground, though, you not only know
the trails; each of them is filled with stories to keep you
company.

Nick and I end our day's wander, for instance, at
Route 9N, the road that connects the metropolis of
North Creek with the bustling communities of Minerva
and Newcomb. In point of fact, a dog could nap quite
nicely on this road. But if that dog had been napping
there one night in 1901, he would have had a tale to tell.
Theodore Roosevelt was vacationing in the Adirondacks
that summer. These mountains were old stomping
grounds of his (his first publication was a bird list of the
Adirondacks), and as governor he'd done much to protect them. Now he was vice president, and climbing
Mount Marcy on his holiday, when word came that
President McKinley, shot by an anarchist earlier in the
summer at the Buffalo World's Fair, had taken a sharp
turn for the worse. A guide charged up the mountain to
tell TR, who hurried back down to find a stagecoach

waiting at the trailhead. A mad night drive down this road brought him to the train station at North Creek[4]—and there he learned that McKinley had died and he was in charge, the mud of the High Peaks still on his boots. And thus began the greatest environmental presidency of our history, the one that saw the protection of more wild places than any since.

Most of the stories passing through my head were more personal, though. The next day, for instance, after a spell of dirt-road walking, I was alone on the trail into a place called Blue Ledges. But not really alone. I could remember carrying my godson Micah on my shoulders through here years ago, and remember how proud I was of my Sophie, only a couple of years older, when she made the same hike uncomplaining. Halfway down the trail I started to hear a dull roar off to my right, and I knew just what it was: the Hudson falling over the rapids at Blue Ledges. And I knew that when I got there it would be—always is—drop-dead gorgeous.

Most people recognize the Hudson from its wide industrial terminus in Manhattan, or perhaps as a broad foreground for the slope-shouldered Catskills of the Lower Hudson Valley (that's where the Hudson River School met). But here you could throw a rock across the river with ease—it's only twenty or so miles from its

4. In subsequent years the entrepreneurial driver of that stagecoach reportedly sold as souvenirs many dozen horseshoes that his team had allegedly worn that night.

birthplace, a fresh and lively cataract. At Blue Ledges the river takes a sharp turn—there are rapids on either side, but right here just some quiet pools, with fish rising. Froth from the upstream rapids turns in slow, lazy circles, and high above them on the cliff walls that give the place its name, ravens turn in slow, lazy circles of their own, against a translucent half moon in the bright blue mid-morning sky. Lazy seems to be the leitmotif, so I lie down on a broad shelf of rock next to the water and take a nap.

Half an hour later, when I wake, my feet are wet. Which can only mean one thing: the bubble! In the early spring, melting snow pushes more than enough water through the gorge of the Hudson—the rapids fill with enormous standing waves, huge sucking hydraul-ics and holes. But the rest of the year, the rafting indus-try requires a bit of a boost. Three mornings a week, around 10:00 a.m., upstream in the town of Indian Lake, a town employee opens the gate of the dam on Lake Abenaki and lets a surge of water out. As that bubble pushes through, the water rises all through the gorge and then, after an hour or two, subsides again. For those cou-ple of hours the river is big again, big enough to be an exciting raft trip for the paying customers whose whoops and hollers even now I can hear in the distance. This gorge is some of the best white water in the East, and almost certainly the most remote—I've just come in on the one trail, and it stretched a few miles to a dirt road that sees almost no traffic. Cell phones and radios don't work down here in the bottom of the canyon; if you get in trouble, you stay in trouble for quite a while. Every couple of years someone dies, which only adds to the allure.

Still, you could say it's not precisely exactly one hundred percent wild. At least not for the hour that the bubble is coming through. And indeed in the last year or two a few fishermen have begun to complain, loudly, that the daily releases of water are killing life in the stream—that the daily raising and lowering of the stream level, the rapid fluctuations in temperature, kill off invertebrates and hence the trout that rely on them. They've forced the state to convene a series of meetings, which in turn are attended by platoons of raft guides, raft bus drivers, bartenders who pour drinks for raft customers. And environmentalists, hopelessly confused by the whole thing. Are we for the most natural Hudson imaginable? Or are we for the least intrusive tourism imaginable—one that transforms any section of the gorge for just an hour a day, leaves no discernible trace, and provides pretty good jobs for all sorts of people, not to mention converting tens of thousands of people annually into friends of the river? It was only three or four decades ago that people fought an epic battle to keep this same gorge from being dammed for hydropower—shouldn't we be keeping our eye on the real threats?

All this environmentalist knows is that today he's not thinking about it. Today he's going for a ride. I've arranged with friends who run a rafting company to pluck me off the rocks at Blue Ledges and float me the rest of the way down to North River. Boots off! Barefoot! The family party I join has already come through the three miles of rapids on the Indian, where rafts put in, and they've managed the first big drops along the Hudson—they look determined, a tad shell-shocked. The guide steering our raft is named Critter—at least that's his river name, and probably his winter name, too, when he works at the nearby downhill ski resort. He's good—not just at steering, which gets fairly routine, but at the patter that keeps people laughing, not too nervy. We shoot through the long wave train downstream from Blue Ledges, and past Kettle, and Gunsight In and Gunsight Out, and Harris Rift, which has a big hole known to all as the Soupstrainer. Things flatten out eventually, and there's time to jump over the side and swim, or lie back against the big rubber pontoons and watch the mountains slide by on either side.

I've seen this gorge at every season save the dead of winter—one time, pushing for a late-fall trip, we had to hack through several inches of shore ice upstream even to put boats in the water. It's most spectacular in the spring with the water roaring, and most gorgeous in the fall when the hardwoods that wall the sides have turned color. But midsummer it feels just right, the water warm enough and low enough that the rapids are a pleasure instead of a mild peril, the day stretching so lazily out in front of you that there's no hurry (save to keep up with the bubble—if you drop off its back you end up pushing your raft over shallow spots). We drift down to the last sizable rapid, Bus Stop, and then paddle back hard to see if we can "surf" in its never-ending break. And we can! Laughing, soaked, stuck inside the power of the river for a minute or two before we finally pop out and start drifting down again. When the first sign of civilization appears—an old, abandoned railroad bridge that once carried trains headed for an iron mine near the heart of the High Peaks—it's, as always, a bit sad. Tom Sawyer done for another day. Soon we reach the takeout spot, where the river joins the two-lane blacktop of Route 28. We hoist our raft up the bank and onto its trailer, and then we strip off life jackets and helmets and change into dry clothes and drink Coca-Cola and feel more or less perfect in the late afternoon sun.

By now I'm close enough to home—two leisurely days' walk, twenty minutes' drive—that I know half the people in cars driving by. (Adirondackers aren't particularly into Subarus, and there's not enough money for SUVs to dominate. It's pickup country, and most of them actually have something in the bed—a chain saw, a load of firewood—that you wouldn't want to pile in the backseat.) Everyone stops to ask if I want a lift, and so I have to explain my mission over and over, and most of them think it sounds pretty ambitious, since, after all, Vermont is, like, a whole other place. But I'm feeling fine: I've had a day of free mileage, floating instead of walking.

The raft dropped me off right at the confluence of Thirteenth Lake Brook with the Hudson, and I follow it uphill for several miles, right past the entrance to the garnet mine. People have been mining garnet here for more than a century, and though this is the only pit left open, it remains the area's prime employer. The garnet isn't gem-quality; instead, it's turned into sandpaper, or into a fine powder used for grinding TV screens. As mining operations go, it's environmentally benign; far from being toxic, the tailings are used by the county to make pavement, and so at night your headlights often catch a red sparkle from the road. Eventually the brook reaches Thirteenth Lake. Despite its drab name, Thirteenth Lake is a gem—long and narrow, with tall Peaked Mountain climbing above it to the west. The eastern shore houses several dozen expensive vacation homes and the Garnet Hill cross-country ski lodge—but they were all built so cleverly that you can't see them from the water. As subdivisions go, it's as nifty as the mine.

The houses line only half the lake, though—the southern half is part of the Forest Preserve, a vast 100,000-plus-acre chunk called the Siamese Ponds Wilderness. Though it's only a tiny fraction of the public land in the Adirondacks, it's nearly as large as all the protected wilderness in Vermont combined. We're in my town of Johnsburg now—one of the biggest townships in the state, though with one of the smallest populations, a town with forty peaks over 2,500 feet, only two of them with trails. And only a couple of trails connect the various lakes and ponds that dot the Siamese. For the most part you're on your own (in fact, if you come from the east, you have to figure out a way to cross the Sacandaga River, which forms a tough boundary for fifteen or twenty miles. There aren't any bridges, just a couple of cable crossings where you can climb a tree, hang from a strap attached to a carabiner, and try to zip across a wire).

The main trail across the top part of the Siamese wilderness starts at an orange gate, planted there to keep snowmobiles, ATVs, even mountain bikes out. These barricades aren't universally popular—I've come across such gates elsewhere in town after they've been dismantled by four-wheeler enthusiasts with acetylene torches. They call them elitist, demand the right to use every inch of the forest, too. The debate usually turns on questions of fact: Do ATV tires turn trails into muddy wallows? But for me the answer is much more basic, having to do with what it means to be civil, a good neighbor, a part of a community. There might be a hundred of us out on this trail today (there aren't, but there could be), and we would barely disrupt one another's experience. Just as Thirteenth Lake can easily absorb a hundred canoes and each of them hardly notices the others. But put one Jet Ski turning doughnuts on the lake, or one four-wheeler careening along the trail, and everyone else's blood pressure starts to rise.

I have an economist friend, Charlie Komanoff, who wrote a long paper proving this point by demonstrating how, say, housing values declined along noisy shores. But in fact it hardly needs proving—only in relatively recent times have people decided that "because I want to" is sufficient reason for annoying others. Only in a culture of hyperindividualism would it occur to you to do what you wanted without reference to anyone else—an Iroquois would have been unlikely to decide that standing in the middle of camp singing at all hours was a good idea, and if he'd made the mistake, the rest of his tribe would have put him straight. But stand on shore someday and listen to the selfish grating whine, hour after hour, of an inboard Jet Ski engine—that's the sound of a culture spinning out of control.

And of course it takes more-tangible forms than noise, too. It wouldn't have occurred to that same Indian to fish all the fish out of a stream—he operated in a world of sharp taboo that made such a thought impossible. But we don't. I was hiking today with John Passacantando, an old friend who'd come to Thirteenth Lake for his summer vacation. John runs Greenpeace USA, which means he spends his time trying, somehow, to shame those who are most egregiously hogging the world's resources, the multinational equivalents of a jerk on a four-wheeler. He sends boats out to block factory fishing fleets strip-mining the ocean with vast nets, and hires climbers to hang banners from the smokestacks of the worst polluters. As we walked, he told me about their latest exploit: his team dressed up in three-piece suits and infiltrated the Exxon Mobil annual meeting, jumping up to shout their anger at the way the company has stone-walled any efforts to even begin addressing global climate change. John and I were arrested together once, along with a couple of dozen other people, in the Capitol Rotunda—our crime was holding up a sign that said STOP GLOBAL WARMING: STOP CAMPAIGN CONTRIBUTIONS FROM GLOBAL WARMERS. We were lucky: the judge thanked us for our "necessary" activism, fined us ten dollars, and said he hoped he'd see us again. We got to walk away feeling righteous.

But that righteousness only goes so far. Because—unlike Jet Skis—we all benefit from the systematic abuse of the planet. Cheap food and cheap energy and cheap wood let us eat big meals, build big houses, drive big cars. In some sense, our entire species, or at least the affluent portions of it, are circling the planet on Jet Skis, careening our four-wheelers through every acre of every continent. In our carelessness we now threaten to raise the very temperature of the planet five degrees. Vroom is us.

I'm as implicated in that as most people. Or almost—I've made modest efforts to rein myself in. We decided on one child; we drive a little hybrid car; we built a house of model efficiency, powered largely by the sun. All that has meant, in certain ways, a lower "standard of living," though by comparison with most human beings I'm still a wild drain on the planet. At best I've gone from vroom to a dull roar. But here's the point: what I've done, in my daily life and my political work and my writing, I've done because of these woods, these very woods we're walking through. They captured my imagination and taught me, in my twenties, that the suburban life I'd grown up in was not as engaging as life out here. I fell in love with these hemlocks, these steep slopes, these patches of rock, these streams lit by leaf-filtered sun. And having fallen in love, the usual braided combination of selfishness and selflessness led me to try to do what I could to protect them. Where I lived, the woods had already been preserved from simple destruction—the Adirondacks are the most legally well-protected landscape on Earth. But even the New York State constitution can't stop acid rain, can't stop rising temperatures, can't stop all the other assaults that drift across the park borders. So that's where I've spent my life, working (with little obvious effect) on global problems like climate change. Were I a better person, I'd tell you that the deepest motivation has been worry for the people of low-lying Asian nations, or fear that we're triggering new waves of malaria, or some one of the thousand other more clearly moral concerns. But mostly it's because of these yellow birches, the bear who left that berry-filled pile of scat, those particular loons laughing on this particular lake.

For me, then, one of the reasons for wild places is so other people can fall in love with them—because surely there are others wired like me, for whom this landscape will be enough. Enough to reorient their compass in a new direction, too. Most of the time now we live under a kind of spell, a lulling enchantment sung by the sirens of our consumer society, telling us what will make us happy. That enchantment is a half-truth at best—you don't need to look very hard at our culture to see that deep happiness is not its hallmark. But breaking that spell requires something striking. For some, it requires seeing how poor people really live, or understanding the depth of our ecological trouble. Or, maybe better, it requires seeing other possibilities, the kind of possibilities I've been describing on this trip. A world where neighbors provide more for each other, growing food and bottling wine and making music, a world where we could take our pleasure more in the woods than in the mall. A world where hyperindividualism begins to fade in the face of working human and natural communities.

That may sound airy and unlikely. Still, for me it has been so, and not just for me. Some years ago, determined to actually collect a few of those oral histories that I never seem to get in time, I sat down with one of my favorite neighbors, Donald Armstrong. He was born in

1918 and, with the exception of his years in the service, never lived anywhere but Johnsburg. I met him first at church, the backwoods Methodist church that serves our tiny town—he and his wife Velda sat in the same pew, six back on the right, week in and week out. (One day, after we'd been taking down the storm windows in the sanctuary, we crawled up into the steeple of the church, and found a place where he'd carved their initials sometime in the late 1920s; they'd been going together since grade school.) When the church celebrated its 150th anniversary, we put together a booklet listing everyone who'd ever belonged, and forty-eight of them were named Armstrong. His father had been a garnet miner—he would drive a team of horses across the then-open fields of the area, and when he found a likely patch of rock he would make a fire, set up a little boiler, and use it to run a steam-powered jackhammer so he could prospect for the ruby ore. When I asked Don what they did for fun in his youth, he talked about baseball and about swimming, but he also said, "In those days, well, they got out to work before daylight. They done chores sometimes with a lantern. They had to work pretty hard. But after the supper meal was over with, my mother would get the dishes caught up and then we'd all move into the front room and my father would tell old stories. Instead of being like we are today with a TV, he'd tell us all the experiences he used to have as a boy." That was it. A limited life, no question.

Don worked in the woods, and he worked building the big mine at Tahawus. When I asked him to recall the single favorite memory of his life, he started talking about this trail I was walking with John today, the trail that branches by the Siamese Ponds. "It's seven miles back in there, you know, so you don't get a lot of riffraff, or a lot of city tourists. Anyway, I was drafted into World War II, and I got the notice I had to report on June 3, 1942. So Velda and I went in to Siamese Ponds. Bert and Celia Nevins, they was in there and had a tent set up. He'd gone ahead and cut ice the winter before, and put it on sawdust, so he could keep your fish cold. We went in and stayed twelve days, cost us a dollar a day. And Celia cooked the best meals. Bert would come out and holler, 'Dinnnnnnnner,' it would echo up and down the lake. She had hot biscuits and potatoes and gravy and trout and tea and coffee. Back insofar and everything, that was about the best meal you ever had.

"I used to tie my own flies. I'd get the feathers out of our chickens' tails, and I used to dip them in gasoline and paraffin wax. That gasoline dissolved the paraffin so it went into a liquid. The gas would evaporate when you'd snap your fly, and then when it went out it would just lay there. Up would come a fish, and you'd shake the pole to make it rattle. Velda was fishing with worms, getting lots of nice panfish. But then she said, 'I'll try the flies.' Well, I hated to let her take the pole, I was having so much fun. But I said okay. I was wearing a railroad cap, and she was whishing that fly back and forth, backcasting you know, and she caught that cap and sent it the whole length of that line. And the next time she cast back and she hooked a fish behind her and didn't know it, and she just twitched that trout right out and sent it the whole length of the line too, kerplunk." A memory, one supposes, that helped sustain him through the European campaign that followed.

To my mind, Donald Armstrong has lived a nearly perfect life—good to his neighbors and loved in return, good to his wife and cherished in return, in a place that meant something to him and where he meant something. Doubtless he made less money than he could have almost anywhere else, but doubtless it didn't bother him, since he had a little house with a little pond out back where he would feed the fish, and a huge garden that entertained and fed him in equal measure. And always always the woods and the mountains and the lakes. He told me about climbing Crane Mountain, our most massive local peak, in his youth: "We were full of beans and buckshot. We'd take that mountain at first speed. And then we'd climb the fire tower up on top, and we'd just look off. All those High Peaks in the distance. It was just amazing to us young people to see off, because we'd never been anywhere out of Johnsburg."

That's an almost incomprehensible idea now, to climb a mountain for a view of the larger world. We see it on TV every hour, or through the Net, or by car and airplane and a thousand other ways. Our worlds are inconceivably bigger—even this sixteen-day journey of mine covers what we think of as a tiny territory, one crossed in a car in a couple of hours. But that doesn't mean that the world I sort of know, or at least apprehend, is more complete or important than the much smaller world he has known. You can have a sufficiency of knowing, just as you can have a sufficiency of stuff.

Or more than a sufficiency. John Passacantando and I have been walking and talking for hours now, but the longer our trek stretches, the quieter we grow. We're along the east branch of the Sacandaga now, rock-hopping, watching the water play. The *abundance* of it all! And the endless novelty—I have hiked these trails in the late fall, when with the leaves down you can read the swell of the ridges with an anatomist's precision. I've skied them dozens of times in the winter—sometimes in heavy glop, sometimes on icy crust, each trip utterly its own. And I've come through here in the muddy spring, skunk cabbage pushing up through the last drifts, river at full throttle. I know people here who are passionate birders or fishermen; I know a woman obsessed with moss and lichen. Trappers and hunters (meaning, if they are any good, people who have taught themselves to think as animals think). Photographers, peak baggers, mushroom nuts. There's a guy who loves to find wild beehives—he tracks the bees in his garden deep back into the woods. Sugar-makers, and paddlers. One local wired the swamp around his home with dozens of microphones so he could record all the sounds of the wetlands. I know another guy who located dozens of apple trees, once growing in farmyards and now, generations later, surviving deep in the woods—he'd prune them, and go back in late summer for his harvest. Only one or two of these neighbors are affluent by the standards of contemporary American consumer society, but every one of them is affluent. I think people who don't know the woods very well sometimes imagine it as a kind of undifferentiated mass of greenery, an endless continuation of the wall of trees they see lining the road. And I think they wonder how it could hold anyone's interest for very long, being all so much the same. But in truth I have a list of a hundred places in my own town I haven't been yet. Quaking bogs to walk on; ponds I've never seen in the fall (I've seen them in the summer—but that's a different pond). That list gets longer every year, the more I learn, and doubtless it will grow until the day I die. So many glades; so little time.

SOMETIMES I GET to cross something off, however. Today, for instance, which is the very last day of this journey. The trail through the Siamese Ponds wilderness ended at Route 8, the north-south two-lane that cuts through our township. It's about the loveliest road I know—glimpses of the Sacandaga again and again as you drive south toward Speculator. And it's also about the loneliest. There aren't any towns for twenty-five or thirty miles south of Bakers Mills. Or rather, there are a couple of towns but no one lives in them anymore. Ghost towns out West desiccate, preserved by the arid sun. Ghost towns in the central Adirondacks (Griffin is the one I know best, an old tannery town just south of here abandoned near the turn of the century) simply rot, cellar holes filling with birch trees, the forest reclaiming its own.

I walk down Route 8 about a mile, just one log truck passing me, and then cross over, heading east into the woods along a short trail to Kibby Pond. Two old and dear friends are waiting for me. Peter Bauer just may be the most effective conservationist in the Adirondacks. For a long time, it was outsiders who saved this place: rich New Yorkers who looked upon it as their vacation paradise and so exerted the power to draw the Blue Line, amend the constitution; many of the locals were bitter, resentful. But with each generation that feeling mellows some, and Peter has built a group, the Residents Committee to Protect the Adirondacks, that speaks with complete credibility on behalf of the park and the people who inhabit it. Steve Ovitt, who I've known almost since the day I came here, looks like a forest ranger even when he's not in uniform—he's clean-cut, broad-chested, strong-shouldered. Steve works for the state Department of Environmental Conservation, and he's responsible for a vast tract of land centered on this forest. We've hiked and winter-camped all through these woods; he's taken me along on all-night searches for lost hunters and lost hikers and lost kids; there's no one I feel more comfortable with in the woods.

Which is good, because today we're leaving the trail altogether. After the quick hike into Kibby Pond, the path ends and we will bushwhack across the top of the Wilcox Lake Wild Forest, another hundred-thousand-acre chunk, and one with just as few trails and even fewer visitors than the Siamese Ponds Wilderness I've just come through. On the other side, seven or eight miles away, is the house where I've spent most of my adult life, but I've never made quite this trip. Nor for that matter has Peter, or even Steve—the woods is a big place.

As we start our wander, Steve is telling stories of his summer so far. Most of it's been spent out West, leading the state's firefighting crew that annually flies out to help in the battle against the biggest blazes on the vast national forests. Invariably they're met with a certain amount of bemusement—what could New Yorkers know about forests? "I just tell them Teddy Roosevelt was our governor before he was president, so we have state land, not federal land," says Steve. As it turns out, the New York crew are regarded as crack firefighters by the bosses at fire command in Boise—this summer Steve was in charge of five miles of fire line on the Crazy Horse blaze near Glacier National Park in Montana. He was calling in bull-dozers, coordinating air attack—and flagging the drive-ways of houses whose location, or cedar shingles, made them indefensible. "You can't have timber to your door-step," he says. "There or here."

Which is an interesting point. Because it's usually so wet, the Adirondacks have a reputation as an "asbestos forest." But Steve got his expertise right here, battling stubborn small fires in piney ledges around the park. "We have a thirty-year fire cycle, and we're forty years into it," he said. "We're due—the incidence of small fires is up every dry year now. The fuels are built up." I've fought Adirondack fires with Steve a couple of times—hacking away at duff with a mattock, sprinkling water from the Indian can carried on my back. Their smoldering persistence is uncanny, a little unsettling—you think you've got it out, and then it's up and running again. And fire in the Adirondacks seems to favor steep, hard-to-reach spots. "Compared to this stuff we're whacking through right now, the West is a walk in the park," says Steve. "That land is all open out there. If I got a crew of those guys out here, they'd be having a fit right now, talking about being in the jungle."

Indeed, the witch hobble was thick on the ground. Not only that, but it's awfully easy to get turned around in these woods once you leave the trail. Even if the sun is out, it's usually hidden by the trees; beavers make last year's small stream into this year's big marsh. I'm competent with a map and compass, but not competent enough. (That is, I almost always find where I'm going, but I have to worry every step of the way that I might not.) So it's a pleasure for me and Peter both to be walking with Steve, who never gets rattled even if he does get turned around.

TODAY HE'S GOT one site he wants us to see on our meander, an illegal hunting camp he discovered some years ago on state land not too far from Kibby Pond. During the fall season, hunters can get permits to set up temporary outposts deep in the woods: a platform tent, usually, that stays up for six or seven weeks and serves as a base of operations. But sometimes sportsmen decide they want something a little fancier, and so they build permanent cabins—and these woods are big enough that without real detective work you're unlikely to come across them. Steve's predecessor as ranger hadn't been especially aggressive in his patrols, and so for the first few years of his posting, Steve had easy pickings—many hunting camps where he either surprised and arrested the occupants or, finding them unoccupied, waited till the ground was safely covered with snow and simply burned them down. This one had been particularly grand: a nice wooden floor, a woodstove, windows out over a small marshy pond. A mile from the trail, in a place that the builder must have been sure no ranger would ever bother to visit. When Steve found it, he staked it out for a while; finally, when he couldn't catch the builder, "I chopped up the floor and poured a lot of Coleman fuel everywhere. When I lit it, it took the roof right off." Now a few charred timbers remain, as a reminder to anyone else who might get the cabin-building bug.

Which is not to say Steve is against hunting—he's about the most enthusiastic hunter I know. Or Peter Bauer, either, though that's often the caricature of environmentalists. The Adirondacks were first protected by an alliance that included hunters and fishermen as well as backpackers and birdwatchers; class and culture have tended to separate that coalition in recent decades, and it's taken a toll, both on politics and, in some ways, on biology. Next to the charred cabin, for instance, we come out on a marshy little beaver flow, hopping from one grassy hummock to the next to keep our feet dry. "This water's so warm—look at that green algae," said Steve. "These brooks used to have all kinds of trout, but that's because people were trapping some of the beavers."

"A couple of decades ago, they'd take 20,000 beavers a year out of the park," added Peter. But the demand for beaver pelts has dropped past the point where not much of anyone wants to trap them anymore, and so the dams proliferate everywhere. Which is not such a good thing for brook trout, who can't tolerate the warm still waters.

Of course, you might be able to help the system more directly by reintroducing the timber wolf, the most important animal that has yet to return to the Adirondacks. Wolves are strong enough to tear through the tops of beaver lodges—they're almost the only effective predator the animal has. But . . . so far efforts to reintroduce the wolf have stalled, largely because hunters worry that they will kill too many deer, too many being defined as "deer that *I* was going to kill."

Nothing is easy, not politics or biology, when the question is how to recalibrate a balance inevitably altered by our presence. I've watched state officials poison everything in an Adirondack pond with a chemical called rotenone. It's designed to wipe out all the "trash fish" like perch, so they can be replaced with "native" trout. (No one really knows which trout were native to which waters, however; and anyway, anglers with bait buckets full of minnows usually manage to reintroduce the other species inside a decade. Some ponds have been poisoned three or four times.) Or say you did reintroduce the wolf— what if the main effect was to make life hard for coyotes, who seem to have filled some of the wolf niche in the Adirondacks, switching their diet to deer and learning to hunt in packs? Do you let forest fires burn? Do you fight them to protect the vacation homes people have built on their fringe? Do you go in and cut the little trees out of the wild so that the fires won't burn as hot? "Management" of anything as complicated as a woods requires more humility than comes easily to our species, at least in its American incarnation.

Still, there are a few things one can say with some confidence. At the moment, in both the Adirondacks and Vermont, one of them is: keep the ATVs out of the forest. Yesterday I made a philosophical argument, but today, walking with Peter Bauer, I get a small update on the down-and-dirty facts. Dozens of volunteers from his Residents' Committee have been monitoring the situation across the park, and uniformly they report the same thing: the four-wheelers are ignoring every rule and regulation designed to control them, and they are turning trail after trail into a rutted, muddy mess. No surprise, really: he tells us about the ads they've collected from off-road magazines. "The basic message is 'Get Muddy,'" he says—every picture shows the big machines leaping over boulders and plowing through ponds. In Japan, where the companies that build them are located, users are restricted to a few privately owned tracks, sort of like our go-kart circuits. But here, until a recent state ruling banning them on the forest preserve, users have been claiming the right to take them anywhere, and arguing, in a parody of political correctness, that restrictions on their use discriminate against people who can't hike.

"People say, 'I'm too old, I can't get where I used to,'" says Steve. "To me, you get a certain amount of time, and then you get your memories. And if you're driving in to some place on your ATV, you're messing it up for the people who are making their memories now."

BY NOW—MIDAFTERNOON—we're completely enclosed within the kingdom of my memories. We've crossed the trail to Fish Ponds (what did I tell you about names?) and we're climbing up an unnamed stream toward a height of land on the shoulder of Ross Mountain. We're seeing lots of bear scat, which leads to bear stories. Steve tells about spending an anxious hour with a big guy a few miles south of here; I show the place where I surprised one while carrying my toddler daughter years ago. We watched it amble away—for us, ever since, the unnamed creek has been Bear Stream. This is deep woods now, but I know a place right off the brook where a cellar hole reveals an old farmstead. There's an apple tree there, and, even better, a hop vine, still bearing a century after anyone stopped harvesting—I cut some of the bitter flowers once and brewed beer with them. There's the yellow birch where our old dog Barley once treed a raccoon and then sat there, calmly, for two hours watching her like she was the movie of the week. There's the slope where I kicked over a yellow-jacket nest and came away with seventy stings. Here's a weird rock—a big boulder with a hole through it almost as if someone had bored it with a drill. The state geologist, Yngvar Isachsen, came to see it one day, and he looked at it for a long time, and then he said, "Damned if I know how that happened."

We're on our own parcel of land now, the one I bought in my mid-twenties when I left the city, 130 acres that run imperceptibly on to the vast state land. We stop for a moment at the swinging bench Sue and I got for a wedding present—I spent a week tromping around looking for the perfect spot, eventually hanging it here between two white pines, where it offers a perfectly framed view of Crane Mountain. Our daughter's middle name is Crane; by now this place is in us deep.

DOWN THE SMALL trail and out into the cleared field. Once there was a barn here, but it had caved in by the time we arrived, and so the local fire company burned it for practice, all of us in our turnout gear on a cold fall day, amazed by the heat that comes from a "fully involved" building. Now there's just grass, and a small fire pit, where we roast marshmallows and swat no-see-ums in high summer. It's right above the pond—the pond where the otters come a few times a year to play with the dog, the pond of a thousand hockey games. And across the pond, the house, where our daughter had her start, and our books, and our marriage. At dusk on a December night, when you take one last swooping turn around the ice, there's no warmer sight in the world than the yellow light spilling out of the kitchen window through a scrim of icicles.

Not today, though. Today it's hot and we're tired, and a journey is at its end, and so of course beer is in order. A little Saranac pale ale from this side of the lake, and a little Otter Creek copper ale from Vermont—we mix them together and drink a toast to this whole territory, indivisible in my mind anyway. Tall granite, high corn, lofty pines. Big people but not too many.

❉

THIS TREK BEGAN, literally, in Robert Frost's backyard; it ends in the domain of a different poet. Jeanne Robert Foster is hardly known at all, but her life coincided with Frost's; she was born five years later than he, in 1879, and died seven years later, in 1970. Only one book of her poems remains in print, a posthumous collection-cum-biography called *Adirondack Portraits.* In the foreword the great literary critic Alfred Kazin writes of his amazement at coming across her work for the first time, "an astonishing duplicate of Frost's slow-moving, artfully conversational pastorals." But, as he also noted, she lacked his "great ego;" in the end, "she was less interested in poetry than in the world it could report."

That world was the one I'd been walking through the last week. Born near Olmstedville, not far from where I'd emerged from the Hoffman Notch Wilderness, she lived a childhood of deep rural poverty, often "farmed out" to other families to earn her keep when there wasn't food enough at home. And so she'd lived in Griffin, the ghost town down the Sacandaga; and in North River above the Hudson; and here, a twenty-minute walk from our house, even closer up against the side of Crane Mountain.

And then she made an almost miraculous breakout—she was a great beauty and, at seventeen, she wed a man twenty-five years her senior who had met her on vacation and took her south to New York, to Boston, where she found herself, all of a sudden, near the center of American culture both popular and high. A drawing of her appeared on the cover of *Vanity Fair;* soon she was one of the Gibson Girls, supermodels of the day. She next worked her way into journalism, first as a newspaper reporter and then as the literary editor of the *American Review of Reviews,* the largest-circulation serious magazine in the country—she wrote eight or twelve pages of book and poetry criticism for the magazine each month, and then went to Europe to help cover World War I. Back in New York, her headquarters was Petitpas' Restaurant, where her circle included the great portrait painter John Butler Yeats (father of William)—an unfinished drawing of Foster was on his easel when he died, and she took his body to the Chestertown, near Olmstedville, for burial. Later she worked closely with John Quinn as he assembled the greatest collection of contemporary art in America—she became friends with Picasso, Joyce, Eliot, Pound; there's a picture in *Adirondack Portraits* of her teeing up a golf ball in a foursome that includes the sculptor Brancusi and the composer Erik Satie.

But all the time she was writing poems, poems about this small slice of the Adirondacks, and the people and the trees she had known in her youth. She published two collections around the start of World War I—*Wild Apples,* and *Neighbors of Yesterday.* Her biographer, Noel

Riedinger-Johnson, says that the books "completed a trilogy of distinguished literary portraits by American women" that also included Willa Cather and Sarah Orne Jewett. More than that, they left the best record of what life was like in Warren County at the turn of the century, in the decades when conservation was gaining the upper hand and the state was starting to buy up huge tracts of the Adirondacks, letting them revert to wildness.

The first thing to strike a reader was how much more crowded it was—almost Vermont-like in its density. The margins of Crane Mountain, now mostly trees with a few vacation homes, then comprised farms small and large. Most of these were subsistence farms, and the subsistence was bare; the growing season up here is probably forty or fifty days shorter than in the depths of the Champlain Valley; I've seen frosts well past Memorial Day and well before Labor Day. One poem, "The Boiled Shirt," describes a family farming sandy soil on the upper edge of the mountain, where "even the hens were lean from always chasing grasshoppers." A photographer comes to take their picture, the only one they've ever sat for, but as he waits he hears the angry voices of the father and the two grown sons. They're arguing, the wife explains, because

> *Each one of them is bound he'll wear* the shirt
> *We're poor; we never had but one boiled shirt.*
> *I hand stitched it of white cloth; the bosom*
> *Is all little tucks that will hold the starch.*

They've always took turns about wearing it,
But today each one wants to wear the shirt.
I said Pa should have the right; all the brunt
Of the hard farm work always fell on him. . . .
Here they come now. I'm glad I've had my way.
Put Pa in front when you take the picture.
You can see that he's wearing the boiled shirt.

Subsistence farming did not automatically breed "community" or "neighborliness" or any of the other virtues we sometimes imagine; Foster tells of a farm wife up and leaving her husband and five children ("I'm only hands and feet for George, / Someone to put the food on the table, / Someone to have more children for him"), and of the last, abortive, tar-and-feathering in town.

And yet it was a full world, too, absolutely full. She tells about a neighbor, Cy Pritchard, who had heard about Johnny Appleseed, and who decided to do the same thing on a smaller scale—visiting his neighbors, eating their apples, saving the seeds.

He liked Seek-No-Furthers and Gill Flowers and
    Greenings,
Tolman Sweets and Russets, pippins and spice apples.

If you had a Sheep's nose, he'd pick that one. . . .
He'd put the seeds into a little bag and thank you."

She describes wax-on-snow at the height of the syrup run, and the giant elm on Landon Hill, and the old pine tree by the baseball diamond in Chestertown, its roots

So large, so old they were a gallery
For all the tired when the baseball nine
Played Schroon or any other North Woods town.

AND IF JOHNSBURG PEOPLE were not perfect, they did build and protect a key stop on the Underground Railroad ("and on Emancipation Day they / Set candles in the windows to proclaim / that man's triumphant spirit rules his clay"). They had every kind of frolic—skating parties, square dances. People who'd never had security found it—Foster writes about one Irish family, refugees from the potato famine, who wouldn't leave their land even to go to church:

I know you'll think we are queer folks.
We feel sometimes that we are deep in sin;
We're happy to stay home, sit on the stoop,
And look out on our fields of oats and rye
And watch the cows down in the pasture lot,
And sheep and the young lambs up on the hill.
It's strange to you who never wanted land
To call your own that we are filled with fear
That some old spell might sweep it all away.

No spell swept it away. Just slow time, the steady spread of an economy that made these most marginal of hill farms impossible. That filled them first with field pine and birch, and then slowly with real forest, till you need to know where to look to find a sign. (But it's still easy to see the cellar hole on the Putnam Farm beneath Crane Mountain where Foster lived, and the wolf maple that grew outside the kitchen window.)

So—is that sad? In a sense, of course. It's a passing, and passings are sad. If the last grassland sparrow leaves Vermont, its call will be missed. In one poem, Foster imagines the ghosts of the two Putnam brothers, come back to survey their land. Enos, frantic, sees the white house rotting, the beehives gone, the cattle and the sheep missing.

I must find a man who still loves the soil
Walk by his side unseen, pour in his mind
What I loved when I lived until he builds,
Sows, reaps, and covers these hill pastures here
With sheep and cattle, mows the meadow land,
Grafts the old orchard, makes it bear again
Knowing that we are lost if the land does not yield.

His brother Francis is calmer, though; he wants only one thing from his visit, "the scent of sweet fern in the August sun."

I can feel both moods. There is a surpassing glory in our right habitation of a place—it's the orderliness of the college garden, the calm of Mitchell's pasture, the humming industry of Kirk Webster's hives, the sweet draught of Granstrom's wine, the endless slow bounty of David Brynn's forests. *It's the glory of the land and the human making sense of each other.* That conversation has almost died out in our nation, drowned by the roar of thoughtless commerce, pointless ease; that's why it's so fine to see places like the Champlain Valley where you can still hear it going on, indeed hear it growing a little louder.

But here on the western shore, there is another—equal—kind of glory, the glory of the human voice growing quieter and quieter till it's only a whisper. Foster's last poems return, relentlessly, to Crane Mountain, the mammoth, steep-sided hunk of rock, twin-summited with a big pond in the saddle between, its high flanks carpeted with berries and hence fertilized with bear scat. In one verse, two sons ask their father why he sold the family timber lot on one side of the mountain to the state for part of the forest preserve.

> *I gave the mountainside to keep it wild,*
> *Free for the life that it has had so long*
> *The trail will always be what it is now.*
> *The summit, with its scrubby balsam trees. . . .*
> *I listened to the brook. The yellow*

Lady-slipper grows there, and the pink,
And other flowers that fly the feet of men.
I touched the trees; somehow they sing to me;
The pine and hemlock leaning to the wind;
The birdseye maple and, where the sun could touch,
The slippery elm we used for medicine.

There are still two hundred acres of cleared land,
The beaver meadows, and the sugar bush and orchards
For my sons. In future years you will come here
And touch the trees as I have done,
And think that I did right.

Some passings, in other words, are sadder than others. The conversion of a farm into a strip mall or a tract of pasteboard mansions saddens because it's irrevocable, at least on a human time scale; it replaces the particular, the appropriate-to-this-place, with the general, the one-size-fits-anywhere. Whereas the slide of a farmstead or a woodlot into wildness—or vice versa—merely trades one appropriateness for another. It's like the passage of a youth into an adult, a slow change and maturation that, with luck, never strikes the observer as too abrupt or ungainly. And if one is truly lucky the passage from adult to corpse will go as smoothly, seem a natural shift that leaves us sad for what is no more, but not shaken. That renews our sense of the propriety of things. A blur, not a line.

❈

I HAVE THE great good fortune to have found the place I was supposed to inhabit, a place in whose largeness I can sense the whole world but yet is small enough for me to comprehend. If, when it comes my turn to die, I really do see again that view from Mount Abe, I know it will contain all these things: farm, field, forest, mountain, loon, moose, cow, monarch, pine, hemlock, white oak, shepherd, bee, beekeeper, college, teacher, beaver flow, bakery, brewery, hawk, vineyard, high rock, high summer, deep winter, deep economy. Yes, and cell phone tower and highway and car lot and Burger King. This is part of the real world. But what's rare in that real world, and common here, is the chance for *completion*. For being big sometimes and small at others, in the shadow of the mountains and the shade of the hemlocks.

Permissions

Grateful acknowledgment is made to the following for permission to reprint previously published material:

COUNTERPOINT PRESS: Excerpt from "Sabbath Poem Number 2" from *The Timbered Choir: The Sabbath Poems 1979–1997* by Wendell Berry. Copyright © 1998 by Wendell Berry. Reprinted by permission of Counterpoint Press.

SYRACUSE UNIVERSITY PRESS: Excerpts from "The Boiled Shirt," "The Apple-Eater," "The Old Pine Tree," "The Mooneys," "The Brothers Return," and "State Land" from *Adirondack Portraits: A Piece of Time: Jeanne Robert Foster,* edited by Noel Riedinger-Johnson (Syracuse University Press, Syracuse, NY 2003). Reprinted by permission of Syracuse University Press.

Acknowledgments

MOST OF THE PEOPLE who aided me in this trip are described in the text. But of course a book requires assistance from many others as well. They include my colleagues at Middlebury, including Chris Klyza, Steve Trombulak, Jon Isham, Connie Bisson, Helen Young, Pete Ryan, Becky Gould, Kathy Morse, Janet Wiseman, and crucially, Nan Jenks Jay. At Crown, my dear old friend Annik La Farge was her usual wise and cheerful self; I am also grateful to her crack coworkers Mario Rojas, Jackie Aher, and Lauren Dong, and to copy editor David Wade Smith. Justin Allen and Katherine Fausset help make my agent, Gloria Loomis, the finest in the land.

I am most grateful to all the many people who have helped preserve and protect the landscapes described herein. And especially to the two people who have helped me enjoy them most: my wife, Sue Halpern, who captured these places so powerfully in her recent novel *The Book of Hard Things,* and my daughter, Sophie Crane McKibben, who truly is a child of the mountains on both shores of Lake Champlain.

About the Author

BILL McKIBBEN's first book, *The End of Nature,* was also the first book for a general audience on climate change; it appeared in the *New Yorker* and has been translated into twenty languages. His eight other books include *The Age of Missing Information* and *Enough: Staying Human in an Engineered Age.* His work appears frequently in *Harper's Magazine, The Atlantic Monthly, The New York Review of Books, Outside,* and many other national publications and has been widely anthologized, including in the Oxford and Norton books of nature writing and in *The Best American Science and Nature Writing, The Best American Spiritual Writing,* and *The Best American Travel Writing.* A scholar in residence at Middlebury College, he is the 2000 winner of the Lannan Literary Award for Nonfiction.